D0723678

DIVING & SNORKELING
Philippines

Tim Rock

MELBOURNE | LONDON | OAKLAND

Diving & Snorkeling Philippines
2nd edition – April 2010

Published by
Lonely Planet Publications Pty Ltd
ABN 36 005 607 983
90 Maribyrnong St, Footscray,
Victoria, 3011, Australia
www.lonelyplanet.com

Lonely Planet Offices
Australia Locked Bag 1, Footscray, Victoria, 3011
Phone 03 8379 8000 Fax 03 8379 8111

USA 150 Linden St, Oakland, CA 94607
Phone 510 510 250 6400 Toll free 800 275 8555 Fax 510 893 8572

UK 2nd Floor, 186 City Road, London, EC1V 2NT
Phone 020 7106 2100 Fax 020 7106 2101

Author Tim Rock
Sales Manager Sarah Ouellette
Project Manager Ellie Cobb
Designer Yukiyoshi Kamimura
Managing Layout Designer Indra Kilfoyle
Editors Justin Flynn, Louisa Syme, Angela Tinson,
Saralinda Turner, Kate Whitfield
Print Production Manager Graham Imeson

Printed by Hang Tai Printing Company
Printed in China
Photographs Tim Rock (unless otherwise noted)

© Lonely Planet 2010
© Photographers as indicated 2010

All rights reserved. No part of this publication may be reproduced,
stored in a retrieval system or transmitted in any form by any
means, electronic, mechanical, photocopying, recording or otherwise except brief extracts for the purpose of review, without the
written permission of the publisher. Lonely Planet and the Lonely
Planet logo are trademarks of Lonely Planet and are registered in
the US patent and Trademark Office and in other countries.

Although the authors and Lonely Planet have taken all reasonable
care in preparing this book, we make no warranty about the accuracy
or completeness of its content and, to the maximum extent permitted, disclaim all liability from its use.

Although the authors and
Lonely Planet have taken all
reasonable care in preparing
this book, we make no warranty about the accuracy or
completeness of its content
and, to the maximum extent
permitted, disclaim all liability from its use.

Contents

Author

Author Tim Rock

TIM ROCK

Tim attended the journalism program at the University of Nebraska – Omaha, and has been a professional broadcast and print photojournalist for more than 30 years. The majority of those years have been spent in the Western and Indo-Pacific, reporting on environmental and conservation issues. His TV series *Aquaquest Micronesia* was an Ace Award finalist. He has also produced six documentaries on the history and undersea fauna of the region. He has won the prestigious Excellence in the Use of Photography award from the Society of Publishers in Asia. He also lists many other awards for photography and writing, publishes a series of coffee-table books and works as a correspondent for numerous Pacific Rim magazines. He is the author of many Lonely Planet/Pisces Diving & Snorkeling guides including *Belize*; *Bonaire*; *Cayman Islands*; *Thailand*; *South Africa*; *Chuuk Lagoon*; *Pohnpei & Kosrae*; *Bali & Lombok*; *Guam & Yap*; *Palau* and *Papua New Guinea*. Lonely Planet Images (www.lonelyplanetimages.com), Double Blue Images (www.doubleblue .com) and other agents worldwide represent Tim's photographic work.

PHOTOGRAPHIC EQUIPMENT

Tim's photographic underwater equipment comprises Aquatica housings and Nikon digital cameras with Nikon, Tokina and Sigma lenses. Ikelite makes his DS125 strobes. TLC strobe arms are used to angle the strobes. Land cameras are also Nikon. Land flashes are made by Nikon. All photos are taken by and copyrighted by the author unless otherwise noted. No photos may be reproduced in any form without written permission from Lonely Planet, Lonely Planet Images (lonelyplanetimages.com) and Tim Rock/Doubleblue.com.

FROM THE AUTHOR

A warm thank you to my wife Larie for her support and help in my travels and writing this guide. I would also especially like to thank Yoko Higashide for her always invaluable help with modeling, diving and both underwater and land photography.

Thanks also go to Yvette Lee, Allan Nash, Tommy Söderström, Kjell Söderström, Pete Eaton, Jamie Gladwin, Omar Lingsangan, Menchie Almirol, Bryan Kim, Rolf Winkelhausen, Dirk Fahrenbach, Jun Jun Verano, Simon Rathbone, Emily Banagua, Gilbert Suan, Rino Tabangan, Demy Tubil, Arnold Tubang, Ruby and Rodel Lita, Annie Buenaagua, Deo Alcantara, Juliette de la Cruz, Wayne Dicker, Cathy Ridsdale, Mike Nelson, JN Dayday, Botchoy Pino, Tata Roxas, Trevor Holmes, Andrea Agarwal, Bobby Adrao, Danny Felizardo and Ronnie Santa Ana, who all shared some great insights about the Philippines. This is the 2nd edition and I would like to thank initial author Heneage Mitchell for providing solid groundwork on which to base this book.

Also, I would especially thank the people of the Philippines for their hospitality and dedication to the preservation of the marine world that brings such beauty to so many divers.

FROM THE PUBLISHER

The Philippines and its 7000-plus islands comprise one of diving's special places. It is the world's second-largest archipelago. The country and its people have become dedicated to setting up reserves that will aid in the conservation of its bays, reefs and marine resources. We are happy to present this newly updated guide to the snorkel and dive sites of the many thousands of islands within the Philippines. We hope you enjoy the bountiful Philippine natural resources found within this gifted and bustling country.

Schooling bigeye jacks at Tubbataha

Introduction

The Philippines is situated between Indonesia and the western reaches of the Pacific Ocean, and is part of an area known as the Coral Triangle – the world's richest region for coral-reef marine diversity. With more than 7000 tropical islands, the Philippines is one of the great treasures of Southeast Asia. It is a smorgasbord of nature, history and sun-drenched beaches.

The country also has an amazing undersea city of marine residents and is enjoying a renaissance of sorts as diving gains popularity. New dive sites and locales are being discovered and developed, while established dive venues are constantly upgrading, adding marine sanctuaries and expanding services.

This book will introduce you to some of the best and most-popular dive sites in the Philippines. There are literally hundreds to choose from; some people come back again and again to their favorite dive locale while others try a new destination every visit.

We start in the north with Luzon's popular training reefs, the historical shipwrecks (spanning three major wars) in Subic Bay, and Anilao, one of the most-popular dive destinations for the local dive crowd. Next we take a run to beautiful Mindoro, where the above-water scenery is matched by amazing underwater diversity, which makes these reefs an internationally renowned destination for both recreational and tech divers. We'll also visit the Sibuyan Sea for some open-ocean diving and pelagic possibilities.

We will then take you to the Visayas dive sites, which include Boracay with its sugar-white beaches; Malapascua

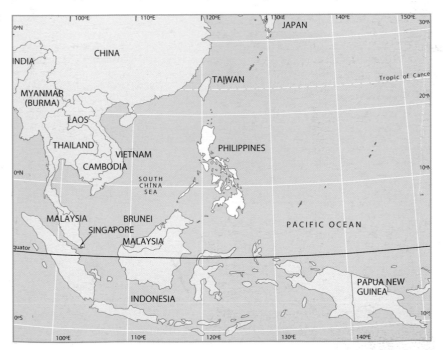

with its mix of reef, wreck and big-critter sites; and Dumaguete, with some of the most fascinating sanctuaries in the country. Cebu City, Moalboal, Bohol and Southern Leyte's offerings will also be explored.

Following that we go to Mindanao, the world's 19th-largest island, known for dazzling scenery and primitive hill tribes. Volcanic Camiguin rises dramatically from the sea and features many coral-laden shoals. The lovely coastal stretch of northern Mindanao also has much to offer.

We finish with the hotbed of nature and diving in the Philippines: the many venues of Palawan, including Apo Reef; and the Sulu Sea. The Calamian island group is just being discovered and Coron has one of the world's best collections of WWII shipwrecks. El Nido is a limestone wonder rivaled only by Thailand's Phi-Phi Island region.

The Philippines has more dive sites than are possible to list in this book, but if you manage to dive all of the sites mentioned here, you'll be doing pretty well. Read through these pages and select the region that appeals most. The country has much to offer from shallow reefs to remote sunken atolls – there's something for every diver.

Plus, the country's friendly people, history and cross section of cultures combine with the diving to make it a can't-miss destination.

THE PHILIPPINES DIVE HIGHLIGHTS

1   **Subic Bay** The relics of war come to the fore with WWII Japanese shipwrecks beckoning the history buff. Grande Island has the coral.
2   **Verde Island Wall** Thick corals and large sea fans highlight this fishy dive off the rocks at scenic Verde.
3   **Apo Island** This Dumaguete area sanctuary boasts nine moored dive sites, all offering healthy corals, sea turtles and lots of fish.
4   **Apo Reef** One of the country's most famous reefs for years, this site offers pelagic action and great coral cover off Mindoro.
5   **Twin Rocks** This Anilao marine sanctuary is good for all levels of divers and offers a chance to see sea turtles, a big school of jacks and giant clams.
6   **Dimyaka Island** Approachable sea turtles, giant clams and even rare dugongs can be found in the waters around this Calamian gem.
7   **Tubbataha Reefs** These reefs and pelagic points in the Sulu Sea can only be seen seasonally, but the amazing walls and big fish shoals make the trip worth planning.
8   **MV Mactan** This former ferry ship is now a fish magnet that divers visit over and over again.
9   **Donsol Bay** The biggest fish in the sea, the whale shark, makes annual appearances here. This place is a must for snorkelers and divers.
10 **Monad Shoal** Get up early to see rare thresher sharks being cleaned by wrasses. Manta rays and hammerhead sharks also come around.

Blue ribbon eel

Gorgonian sea fans and colorful anthias dot a Philippine wall

Facts about the Philippines

Sunny Philippine beach

OVERVIEW

The Philippines is one of the most diverse countries in Asia. It sits along the eastern reaches of Oceania with the Pacific Ocean/Philippine Sea lapping against its east coast and the South China Sea to the west. Indonesia and Malaysia sit south and southwest, while far to the north are Taiwan and China.

The richest coral-reef area in the world, known as the Coral Triangle, is located here. The Philippines is the northern point of the triangle, which also includes Papua New Guinea and Indonesia/Malaysia. This is the cradle of diversity for the world's coral reefs, with more species of both corals and fish found here than any other place in the world.

Within the vast Philippine isles are smaller seas: the Sibuyan, Sulu and Visayan. Each with its own biosphere and characteristics, many odd and unusual creatures have developed and thrived in their own special worlds.

The Philippines also reflects this same unique build above the sea. Some metropolitan areas are among the world's most modern, such as bustling Manila, with its nine million residents. Modern condos, restaurants, shopping centers, theaters and clubs make it one of Asia's trendiest cities. But travel just a few hundred miles away from the city lights and you might find rural infrastructure not much different than it was 200 years ago. There are cultures within cultures here.

Natural disasters such as floods, earthquakes and erupting volcanoes make the place exciting and unpredictable. And controversial situations ranging from militant Muslims in Mindanao to a past airport-arrival assassination in the capital have set the scene for constant and sometimes tumultuous political change.

Yet, amid this seemingly constant display of growing pains and emotions, the country has remained stable and a favorite for travelers. That's because its magnificent rivers, verdant rice terraces, rolling hills, tepid rainforests and scattered islands create a natural sensory overload that overrides the petty struggles of man.

The Philippines has always been a regional dive-destination favorite, and now, with new resorts on newly explored islands popping up while the tried and true get better and better, it is becoming one of the most popular places to visit in the international diving world. Toss in reasonable prices and a usually favorable exchange rate for most of the world's leading currencies and you have a real gem of a country to explore.

HISTORY

One of the big attractions for tourists visiting the Philippines is its long history evidenced in its crafts, old churches, WWII remnants and today's modern designs.

Prior to its first contact with western man and resulting Spanish occupation, the Philippines was an ancient land of farmers and hunter-gatherers.

The first inhabitants of the Philippines arrived up to 300,000 years ago, probably migrating over a land bridge from the Asian mainland. The Negrito, or Aeta, arrived 25,000 years ago, but were driven back by several waves of immigrants from Indonesia, followed by maritime immigrations of Malayan people. In 1380 the Arab-taught Makdum arrived in the Sulu archipelago and began to establish what would become a powerful Islamic sphere of influence over the next hundred years.

Ferdinand Magellan arrived in 1521 and claimed the archipelago for Spain. Magellan was killed by local chiefs who, quite naturally, disapproved of this notion. Ruy Lopez de Villalobos followed in 1543 and named the territory Filipinas after Philip II of Spain. Permanent Spanish occupation began in 1565, and by 1571 the entire country, except for the strictly Islamic Sulu archipelago, was under Spanish control.

A Filipino independence movement grew in the 19th century, and Filipinos fought on the side of the Americans in 1898 during the Spanish–American War. When the Spanish were defeated, General Emilio Aguinaldo declared the Philippines independent. The US, however, had other plans and promptly purchased the islands from the Spanish for US$20 million. The US eventually recognized the Filipinos' desire for independence, and Manuel L Quezon was sworn in as president of the Philippine Commonwealth in 1935 as part of a transitional phase pending full independence. Japan invaded the Philippines in 1942, brutally interrupting this process, and ruled until the US reinvaded two years later. The Philippines received full independence in 1946.

All was calm until Ferdinand Marcos was elected president in 1965. Facing opposition for his policies, he declared martial law in 1972 and ruled virtually as a dictator until 1986. His regime was attacked by both communist and Muslim guerrillas. He was accused of ballot rigging and fraud. The assassination of prominent opposition figure Benigno Aquino in 1983 at Manila's airport – which now bears his name – sparked massive anti-government protests. A snap election in 1986 saw the opposition parties rally around Aquino's widow, Cory. Both parties claimed victory, but Aquino was widely believed to have polled the most votes. She initiated a program of nonviolent civil unrest, which resulted in Marcos fleeing the country to asylum in Hawaii, via Guam, with US Air Force help.

Aquino re-established the democratic institutions of the country, but failed to tackle economic problems or win over the military and the powerful Filipino elite.

US strategic influence in the country diminished following the 1991 Mt Pinatubo eruption, which destroyed the US Clark Air Base and after the Philippine Senate refused to ratify the lease on the Subic Bay Naval Station. Aquino survived seven coups in six years and was succeeded by her defense minister, Fidel Ramos, in 1992. Ramos attempted to revitalize the economy, attract foreign investment, cleanse corruption and expand provision of utilities.

The Philippine government and the Moro National Liberation Front (MNLF) signed a peace accord in September 1996, ending, formally at least, the MNLF's 24-year struggle for autonomy in Mindanao. The peace agreement foresaw the MNLF being granted considerable autonomy in many of the island's provinces. Peace in the area remains elusive, however, following the rise of a splinter group, the militant Moro Islamic Liberation Front (MILF), which opposes the agreement. The government continues to conduct military operations in MILF-held areas in Basilan and Sulu.

In 1998, Ramos was replaced as president by Philippines films' answer to Bruce Willis, Joseph Estrada. Estrada, a former movie star, promised a lot economically – but more-than failed to deliver. He was impeached and brought to trial in late 2000 on charges of taking bribes from gambling syndicates and using the proceeds to line his own dens and to build extravagant houses for his mistresses. When Estrada and his political allies tried to derail the trial by blocking prosecutors' access to his financial accounts, the people decided they'd had enough and staged mass demonstrations in the streets of Manila.

Estrada finally threw in the towel on January 19, 2001, and the next day his former vice president, Gloria Macapagal Arroyo, was sworn in as the new president of the Philippines. In an inauguration speech that must have sounded eerily familiar to the people of the Philippines, Arroyo promised to wipe out poverty and corruption. At the time of writing she was spearheading a number of civic-improvement and tourism campaigns, including those aimed at developing sport diving in the country.

DIVING HISTORY

In the Philippines, the birth of sport diving is generally credited to the pioneering efforts of Aquatropical, which opened its doors to divers in Anilao in 1966. That makes this country one of the earliest to found sport diving. Since then, the sport has blossomed. Divers still generally use the traditional bangka outriggers, which gives the sport a nice local touch. But nowadays these bangkas are customized for diving tourists and can be spacious, comfortable and easy to use with big dive ladders, a head and even a kitchen.

At the same time, divers are also being ferried by modern fiberglass dive boats with all of the safety features found in developed destinations. Tech diving has also gained a lot of ground in the Philippines and, in some cases, has become a prominent form of diving. Depth records and lots of specialized training have made it a leader in the technical aspects of the sport. Tech divers travel from all over Asia to embrace the Philippine waters for a chance to see the ocean's deeper reaches.

The future of diving looks good – more and more sanctuaries are being established as the promotion and conservation of sea life gains momentum as people see it translate into tourism-related jobs.

GEOGRAPHY

This is where things get really interesting. Mountains, rain forest, rice terraces, volcanic cones and sandy isles and atolls can all be found in this rich mixed bag of regions and features.

The islands: only about 1000 are larger than 0.4 sq miles (1 sq km); only 2000 have inhabitants; 2500 or so don't even have mapped names; the official count is 7107 islands. Luzon and Mindanao are the largest islands, together comprising 66% of the country's land.

About half the country is under cultivation and there are active volcanoes in the Philippines – ancient eruptions are responsible for the extremely fertile soil. Luzon's northern mountains produce an array of fruits and vegetables, while the ash-rich plains north of Manila are the country's major rice producers. Most of the islands were formed by past and current volcanic and tectonic activity.

A third of the country is still forested, despite the continued practices in some areas of unsustainable forestry

CLIMATE

The Philippines has consistently warm and humid tropical weather with pronounced wet and dry seasons. The rainy season is typically considered to be from July to October, with the dry season being November to June. This varies, as it is dictated by the *amihan* (northeast monsoon) and the *hagabat* (southwest monsoon).

It is said that temperatures average about 70°F (22°C), but that average must take into account the Baguio Mountains, because it is normally warmer at beach level across the country. The hottest months are from March to May, when big-cement-city temperatures in Manila hit a scorching 95°F (34°C) and warm winds bathe the beaches. Humidity runs at a balmy 70%. The coolest months are December to February.

POPULATION, PEOPLE & CULTURE

With a population of roughly 78 million, the Philippines' people are as diverse as its ecology. The Filipino is basically of Malay stock with a sprinkling of Chinese, American, Spanish and Arab blood.

The Filipinos are divided geographically and culturally into regions, and each regional group is recognizable by distinct traits and dialects. Tribal communities can be found scattered across the archipelago.

Blow Baby Blow

The Philippines is occasionally a victim of the Pacific Ocean typhoon season, because it sits in what is called the 'typhoon belt'. These storms move in from Micronesia across the Philippine Sea past or over the country and blow themselves out in the South China Sea. They are usually building in strength and size as they cross the Philippine Sea and can cause considerable damage if they do hit the Philippine landmasses.

Generally, July to October is considered typhoon time, although they can happen at any time of the year. They tend to be a bit stronger as the typhoon season progresses.

With rain blowing sideways in winds in excess of 125mph (200km/h), seas are downright dangerous during a typhoon, and runoff and damage to local villages is common. The good news is that after they blow through, the seas are usually glassy calm and the weather nice, as the system sucks all the nastiness with it toward Vietnam or Taiwan.

So bring a good book, in case you get holed up during this time of year.

LANGUAGES

The Philippines is one of the easiest Asian countries to visit for English speakers, as English is spoken, to some degree, just about everywhere. Since most divers also seem to speak a degree of English, communication, dive briefings and getting directions is a fairly painless experience. Signs are normally in both English and Tagalog, or just English.

The other main language is Tagalog, which is also referred to as Filipino. Sometimes English and Tagalog are mixed for a bit of 'Engalog'. Hearing a Filipino talk is a soothing experience – Tagalog is a nice language with lilting accents. There are many major dialects throughout the country and each region has its own sayings, expressions and accents. Some regions even have separate languages quite different from the universal Tagalog. Approximately 111 languages and dialects are spoken in the country. A Filipino can usually pick where another is from just by hearing him or her speak for a minute or two.

GATEWAY CITY

Most people arrive in the Philippines by air and their first experience is in and around Manila. Oh, the traffic! But it gets better once you are out of the hubbub.

This city of some eight million souls has a wide range of hotels and pensions to suit all budgets, as well as some interesting shopping and entertainment options. At places such as the expansive Mall of Asia you can shop, see an IMAX movie, dine and buy a new computer.

The city has a huge variety of restaurants featuring cuisine from around the world. You can visit Christian churches, Chinese temples and Muslim mosques; sail or cruise on Manila Bay, perhaps to the historic island of Corregidor; or just enjoy the famous sunset, spectacular in part because of the light refracting off the omnipresent clouds of pollution.

Puerto Galera kids enjoy their ice cream

Untouched Palawan island

Diving in the Philippines

Hovering over a reef wall

The Philippines is a superb place to get to know the ocean and its creatures. The barrier reefs, marine habitats (such as mangroves) and atolls are said to house some of the most diverse marine creatures in the world.

Whether it's swimming with whale sharks, cruising with manta rays, exploring caves and wrecks or simply hanging out near the awesome walls and reefs, this tropical paradise will fascinate divers of all skill levels and interests.

Philippines dive sites are varied, but they do share some common characteristics. Water temperatures throughout the Philippines fall between 77°F and 82°F (25°C and 28°C), the warmest months being March through June. Though conditions are best between late February and early June, most regions have some diving available year-round. Tidal ranges are generally not more than 3ft (1m) and are usually only a factor with regard to visibility and current.

It pays to check with local dive professionals for advice on currents and other factors before you plan your dive. Dive operators generally take divers to the best site the regions offer, and divers should make every effort to minimize their impact on the reef.

One of the interesting aspects of many Philippine beaches is that there are no piers at the destination, so boats typically go as close to the beach as possible. Divers board and disembark via a wooden plank and have to wade through ankle, knee or chest high water. Bring a dry bag.

In this book you'll find selections that are representative of the vast diversity of sites throughout the Philippines. Many are personal favorites, some are included because they are well known and others may be rarely dived but are just too good to leave out. The depth ranges included with each dive site description indicate where the site's best features are, and a '+' after the range means deeper dives are possible. Be sure to plan your dives and dive your plans – keep an eye on your depth gauge, especially along wall sites.

WHEN TO GO

There are various weather patterns in this part of the world that affect the Philippines, and its important to know when these occur in the particular destination you are hoping to dive. Regional landmasses and mountains may create weather patterns specific to their area.

Most everywhere, sea conditions are affected by the winds, but are considered to be at their best between late February and early June across the Philippine archipelago. But while areas such as the Sulu Sea have a specific calm season (from March to early June), most of the dive regions in the Philippines have good, accessible dive sites year-round.

WHAT TO BRING

The climate in the Philippines is tropical. Light, casual clothes are the norm, but if you will be straying from the beach and heading into mountain regions you'll need a sweater and/or jacket.

When visiting churches and temples, no shorts, tank tops or bikinis are

---

The Best Dives

Beach Dive
The **Club Paradise Housereef** walk-in at Dimakya Island offers a lot of diversity. Look for odd pipefish, feeding turtles and dugongs, cuttlefish and giant clams.

Shark Dives
The best chance to see an unusual thresher shark, with its elongated tail, is at **Monad Shoal** off Malapascua. For whale sharks, in season, **Donsol** is the place to be.

Reef Dive
Apo Island is one of the healthiest and most prolific reef sanctuaries in Asia. Look for healthy hard corals and lots of sea turtles, as well as a big school of jacks.

Park Dive
Tubbataha is a World Heritage Site and a marine sanctuary. The Tubbataha North area offers several fissured sites good for pelagic action in the blue water column. It's world class.

Critter Dive
Spring Bubbles, Anilao has hot springs bubbling through the sea floor on occasion. But the odd bit of debris or an old shoe on the bottom also seem to attract walking devilfish and seahorses as well as lots of other oddities.

Whitetip reef shark

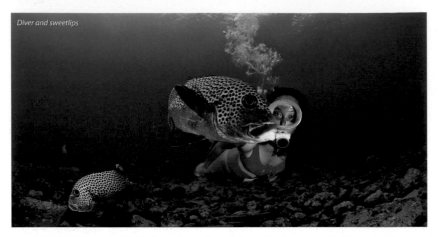
Diver and sweetlips

permitted. Otherwise, it's beach and boat wear by day and maybe some nice, tropical, light dinner clothing for the nicer restaurants. But basically, dress casual and relax. You're on holiday.

WHAT TO BRING DIVING

Another reason the Philippines is a good place to go for a dive trip is because if you do forget something, there are many fully equipped dive shops that offer both rental and sales, including parts purchase such as fin straps, and even some regulator repair. If you're not picky and don't want to carry dive gear, full rental of all kit is also available from many of the sanctioned shops in the country. PADI, SSI and NAUI are the main certifying agencies throughout the Philippines.

The water is tropical and generally clear. Temperatures can range from a bathtub warm, rash-guard suitable 86°F (28°C) to a 3mm-to-5mm-wetsuit-requiring 70°F (21°C) for a couple of months in the winter and at places known for upwellings. But generally, the water temperature is 78°F to 84°F (25.6°C to 28.9°C). Heartier folks just wear skins or T-shirts; while those acclimated, such as divemasters, wear 5mm to 7mm. But for the average tourist, all that is needed is a 1.5mm to 3mm wetsuit to remain very comfortable.

Do NOT bring a speargun. A lot of diving is done in or near the nation's many protected areas and the reefs are already under heavy fishing pressure. The use of a spear on scuba is against the law.

Nitrox is offered more and more. Don't forget your 'C' card and dive log to show to your host dive shop. And bring your mixed gas card if you are going to use Nitrox. Rebreather diving, rental and training is also available in the Philippines.

DIVE TRAINING AND CERTIFICATION

The Philippines is one of the world's best places to learn to dive. The waters are well suited to training requirements, with warm, clear water and shallow coral reefs ideal for beginners, as well as rewarding deep dives, wrecks and caves perfect for advanced and technical training.

You can choose from among literally hundreds of dive centers, most affiliated with the Professional Association of Diving Instructors (PADI), with thousands of qualified instructors eager to advance you to the next level of training. While PADI is the main agency represented, Technical Diving International (TDI) courses are also offered. The Philippine Commission on Sport Scuba Diving (PCSSD) also registers and accredits dive establishments, providing some assurance that registered shops offer quality services. Prices are reasonable and equipment standards are often very high. See the Listings chapter at the back of this book for advice on selecting a dive operator.

There are all levels of training offered, from snorkeling and basic scuba to full instructor courses. Check with your dive shop to see what courses you can take. The Philippines is perfect for Nitrox, advanced courses, marine life courses and many other specialties.

Most costs for diving are pretty much the same across the country. But remember, the cheapest package may or may not be the best and safest training – ask questions and shop around for the best situation for your needs, this is your candy store.

Dive courses are run year-round in the many popular resort areas, so you'll also find ample opportunities to guide divers, assist with courses and learn how to maintain and repair equipment.

LIVE-ABOARDS

There are currently many live-aboards operating around the Philippines, and their popularity seems to be growing, with new routes and venues being offered every season.

The live-aboards provide a very convenient way to see the far-away sites and visit the diverse 'natural parks' such as Apo Reef and Tubbataha. A live-aboard trip is highly recommended for the hard-core diver who wants to see as much as possible of the Philippines' undersea world. They normally offer the usual dive-until-you-drop agenda of four daytime dives and a night dive, interspersed with ample meals and naps. Food can be varied and very good, featuring both international and savory local specialties.

It pays to do a bit of research to see if the live-aboard trip you envision is actually the one being offered. Some can be quite luxurious while others are just a notch above camping; they range from

Live-aboard dive fun

Hard corals and starfish

some very large ships, such as those of the popular Expedition Fleet, featuring weeklong excursions, to smaller, converted bangkas, which are more economical and used for overnight and three-day trips. Some divers enjoy the commune with nature offered by the bangka experience, while others prefer just to dive and have nice air-con creature comforts available afterwards. Shop around to find the best fit for you and what you want both above and below the water.

Also check with your operator to see if any extras are offered, such as free Nitrox or airport transfers.

SNORKELING

Most of the popular reef-diving destinations also have good house reefs and shallow bays that offer snorkelers a place to spend long hours admiring the undersea inhabitants. As the water here is normally clear, especially at high tide, and shore access is easy at many beachside resorts, snorkeling is a very popular pastime. Many local people come to the venues with their families, especially on weekends, for the snorkeling alone.

The reason corals in the Philippines are so healthy is because there is current

flow – be well aware of the currents in the area you wish to snorkel. Also, some places have a lot of small boat traffic. It's very dangerous to snorkel around these lanes, and the fishermen really don't look for, or expect, snorkelers to be there. Carry a flag or a float or, better yet, just avoid the high traffic bangka areas.

Snorkeling can be especially rewarding at wild places with clear water, such as Apo Island and Tubbataha (along the tops of the drop-offs). But make sure your boatman knows where you are, and you both keep an eye on one another, as currents can come up quickly here.

UNDERWATER PHOTOGRAPHY

Underwater photography is the main reason many divers come to the Philippines. The reefs are colorful, the wall dives have beautiful gorgonian sea fans and the diversity of fish and invertebrates is among the best in the world. Many top photographers make the Philippines an annual stop. And many Philippine-based photographers have made international names for themselves photographing the stunning rarities found in their home waters.

The country really isn't that well equipped to handle major photography needs. There are disposable and reusable cameras for sale for snorkelers and shallow divers, and print film is sold at some stores. Electronics shops may also have some low-capacity memory cards for digital cameras. But those with higher-end cameras or professional equipment and digital single lens reflex (DSLR) housings should bring everything they need, including appropriate back-ups, such as spare chargers.

There are a few larger dive centers with a staff pro for instruction or camera rental, or to shoot stills or a personal video of your dive. E-6 processing is now nonexistent, but getting print film developed is easy, so you can check your images regularly if you shoot print film. For digital divers, the power is consistent at most resorts, although at some islands and more remote locales, you may find 'power hours', which means the power is on mostly only at night. You can plug in your laptop and check and edit pictures during this period, as well as charging things up. For this reason, you may want to bring along a power strip (power board) to plug everything into.

Live aboards and a few resorts have dedicated camera rinse and maintenance areas with blowers and charging cubicles. Otherwise, you will have

to set up a charging station and 'editing suite' in your room. Crews at most experienced dive shops seem to be very aware of the cost of larger DSLR rigs and do handle them with care. They will help you get them on and off the ship – this is necessary at times, because you have to board the dive bangkas via a ramp or a smaller boat. Crews are generally also good about handing down the camera when you jump in, and taking your camera back to a secure place after the dive. Just watch to make sure they don't put the housing down on the lens or dome. Odd contraptions such as housed cameras can be confusing, so if you have any specific handling instructions, tell your divemaster so they can relate it to the crew.

Camera rinse buckets vary and range from actual buckets to big, sawed off plastic barrels that can hold many point-and-shoots, a couple of DSLR systems or some video housings. These are excellent for rinsing between dives. Ensure your dive shop has something similar and that it is full of fresh water – nothing like opening up the rinse cooler and finding it is empty. Another problem is that the rinsing of masks and computers is sometimes allowed and encouraged in the camera rinse bucket. Since products such as lens defoggers can affect acrylic, it's best to discuss

Night dive with a frogfish!

what should and should not be done in the camera bucket with the shop manager to ensure fresh water is the only thing getting on your camera.

Also, those with larger cameras and housings may want to handle the cameras themselves. Crews are often eager to help photographers, but this can result in your set-up being crammed into a rinse bucket, scratching a dome or bending a strobe cord. Also, lanyards from smaller cameras can cause latches to become unlatched, resulting in a freshwater flood – it's best to wash your own housing lest some other guest grab their camera and inadvertently open your housing in the process.

In short, there are acceptable facilities that are generally available for camera care. But bring everything you may need for photography, charging and maintenance including back-up chargers. And don't be lazy – handle your gear yourself. You came all this way to make underwater photos, and hauled a lot of gear with you – ensure there's no one else to blame if an accident takes place.

Rating System for Dives & Divers

The dive sites in this book are rated according to the following system. These are not absolute ratings but apply to divers at a particular time, diving at a particular place. For instance, someone unfamiliar with prevailing conditions might be considered a novice diver at one dive area, and an intermediate diver at another, more-familiar location.

Novice
A novice diver generally fits the following profile:
- has basic scuba certification from an internationally recognized certifying agency
- dives infrequently (less than one trip a year)
- has logged fewer than 25 total dives
- has little or no experience diving in similar waters and conditions
- dives no deeper than 60ft (18m)

*A novice diver should be accompanied by an instructor or divemaster on all dives.

Intermediate
An intermediate diver generally fits the following profile:
- may have participated in some form of continuing diver education
- has logged between 25 and 100 dives no deeper than 130ft (40m)
- has been diving within the last six months in similar waters and conditions

Advanced
An advanced diver generally fits the following profile:
- has advanced certification
- has been diving for more than two years
- has logged over 100 dives
- has been diving within the last six months in similar waters and conditions

Pre-Dive Safety Guidelines
Regardless of skill level, you should be in good physical condition and know your limitations. If you are uncertain as to which category you fit into, ask the advice of a local dive instructor. They are best qualified to assess your abilities based on the prevailing dive conditions at any given site. Ultimately you must decide if you are capable of making a particular dive, depending on your level of training, recent experience, and physical condition, as well as water conditions at the site. Remember that water conditions can change at any time, even during a dive.

Conservation

KA-BOOM, TROUBLED ENVIRONMENT

It's pretty hard to spend any time diving in the Philippines without seeing and hearing the result of blast fishing. You might be swimming along and hear a 'plink' noise that sounds like maybe someone's o-ring lost its seal. When you look around and see your buddy is alright, you realize you just heard a dynamite blast from far away. Sometimes it is very loud, very strong and unmistakable, as brazen blasters do their thing near popular dive sites.

The Philippines was, until a few decades ago, rich in marine and timber resources. Unrestricted logging and overfishing – in many cases using illegal techniques such as dynamite, cyanide, muro-ami and drift netting –

have seriously depleted forest, coastal and offshore resources. Coral bleaching resulting from the increased water temperatures of El Niño years has also stressed the marine ecosystem, although most reefs seem to have bounced back quickly from the effects.

There is no shortage of regulations to protect the reefs and fisheries of the Philippines. Spear fishing by scuba divers was declared illegal some years ago, but the law has been relaxed to allow it in some designated areas. Most dive operators, however, have outlawed the practice at popular dive sites, having realized that one live fish is worth far more over its natural life span than the same fish dead on a dinner plate.

Dynamite and muro-ami fishing, fish collection using cyanide and the hunting of marine mammals and whale

The effects of blast fishing are long term: reef rubble on the left and healthy reef on the right

sharks are all banned, but still occur in many parts of the country. Likewise, coral and shell collection is illegal, yet there are still thousands of shell vendors lining the beaches and tourist traps of the Philippines, with their product supplied by subsistence fishermen.

Education is the key and the word is slow to spread. Many fishers don't understand that bombing to feed their families today will ensure that they go hungry tomorrow, and businessmen and politicians, such as regional mayors, also profit from the sale of fish. So destructive fishing continues.

On the brighter side, various environmental groups and government agencies are now teaching communities about sustainable fishing practices. Marine reserves are being established so fish stocks can replenish. Divers also have a positive effect by supporting tourism, which is an alternative source of income for locals. But it is estimated that 90% of the reefs are affected in some way by illegal and damaging fishing methods, so it's still a long road back to health for the entire marine ecosystem to be as it was just a few decades ago.

Heavy ropes from fish traps damage coral

HEALTH & SAFETY

TRAVEL ADVISORIES

Safety can be an issue for travelers in the Philippines, with kidnappings of foreigners, bombing incidents and violence during political demonstrations making international headlines a bit too frequently.

Overall the country's security situation has generally improved in recent years and most of the country is hospitable to travel. However, rebel activity and armed banditry in certain areas of the Philippines poses potential security concerns.

For example, on the southern island of Mindanao, rebels have been fighting for a separate Islamic state within the mainly Catholic country. The decades-long conflict has claimed more than 120,000 lives, and sporadic violence has continued despite a 2003 ceasefire and peace talks. And the Abu Sayyaf group (Muslim separatists) on Jolo, have a history of violence towards hostages. The government has declared all-out war on these rebels.

You can get up-to-date information and travel advisories from the **US Department of State** (www.state.gov) and the **Philippine Department of Tourism** (www.wowphilippines.com.ph).

GENERAL HEALTH

Overall, the Philippines is a healthy place to visit; the main concern is mosquito-borne disease. There is malaria in some of the far-flung provinces but it's not considered a major threat. The real problem is dengue fever, which is also brought to us by mosquitoes and seems to experience outbreaks during the wetter times of the year. To avoid these

Fresh produce from the local market

Safety Tips

In general, the Philippines is a safe place to travel. Crimes against foreigners usually target the unwary and the unprepared. Travelers are advised to exercise good judgment and remain aware of their surroundings. To avoid problems, follow a few general rules:

• Keep your bags with you and in view at all times
• Never accept a drink from a stranger – this is a favorite ploy of drug-and-rob gangs
• Never accept an invitation to join any form of gambling game – you will lose
• If you feel a taxi driver is overcharging you, and you want to dispute the fare, get out of the taxi and remove all your belongings before bringing the matter to the driver's attention
• If it seems too good to be true, it probably is

It is unusual for foreigners to be accosted by officials of the Philippine government, police or armed forces unless the foreigner is obviously behaving badly. If anyone claims to be an official, demands to see your ID or harasses you in any way (especially if they are not wearing a uniform), politely insist on seeing their ID.

Around Manila and in some other parts of the country, Tourist Police Stations are set up to help resolve visitors' complaints – in some cases they can and will help.

illnesses, avoid mosquito bites: use a good repellent and cover up fully when the mosquitoes are active – between dusk and dawn.

PRE-TRIP PREPARATION

There are a number of shops in the Philippines that offer equipment for sale and rental and there is some equipment repair available as well. But if you use your own gear you will want to get your regulator tuned up before coming here if you haven't used it for six months or so. You may also want to do some local check-out dives, even if just in a pool, to check your equipment out.

Also, get some exercise prior to the trip so you can face the challenges of the ins and outs of boat diving, the walks associated with shore diving and the inevitable Philippine currents. Swimming, hiking with a backpack and jogging will help increase fitness and stamina.

Make sure your passport is not about to expire, or already expired. You can't get into the Philippines without one. It needs to have more than six months of eligibility left when you arrive in the Philippines.

DIVERS ALERT NETWORK (DAN) PHILIPPINES

The Divers Alert Network (DAN) is a global network of not-for-profit, member-based, dive-safety organizations working for the safety of all divers through education, research and training.

DAN Asia-Pacific (DAN AP; part of the International DAN Federation of Dive Safety Organizations, with worldwide membership presently exceeding 300,000) provides Worldwide Emergency Evacuation Coverage and optional Dive Injury (Treatment) Insurance services for members. In addition, the organization is responsible for funding and/or manning 24-hour diving emergency hotlines throughout the Asia-Pacific region. DAN does not directly provide medical care; however, it does provide advice on early treatment, evacuation, and hyperbaric treatment of diving-related injuries.

If you ever find yourself in an emergency situation, your first step should be to call the DAN-funded **Diving Emergency Services Medical Hotline** (☎ +61-8-8212 9242). This number is available to all divers throughout the world.

MEDICAL & RECOMPRESSION FACILITIES

Hyperbaric recompression chambers are located in many places in the country.

Recompression Chambers (24-hour emergency service)

Philippine Coast Guard Action Center, Roving Vessel Chamber
☎ 02-527 3880, in Batangas 0917 5362757, 0918 902 1108, 043-723 2745
Contact: Dr Mike Perez; Dr Henry Latonio

Cavite

Sangley Recompression Chamber NSWG, Philippine Fleet Naval Base, Sangley Point, Cavite City
☎ 02-524 2081/5, 02-524 4490
Contact: Capt Pablo Acacio

Cebu

Philippine Commission on Sports Scuba Diving (PCSSD) Office, Cebu
☎ 02-254 9262
Contact: Helen Etcuban

VIZCOM Station Hotel, Lapu- Lapu, Lahug, Cebu City
☎ 032-232 2464/8, 032-233 9942

Contact: Macario Mercado; Mamerto Ortega

Manila

AFP Medical Center, V Luna Rd, Quezon City
☎ 02-920 7183, 02-426 2701
Contact: Dr Jojo Bernardo MD
DAN SE Asia Pacific, Suite 123, Makati Medical Center, 2 Amorsolo St, Makati City
☎ 02-817 5601
Contact Dr Benjamin Luna MD

PCSSD Office, Room 315 Department of Tourism Bldg, Manila
☎ 02- 524 3735, 02-528 4428
pcssddot@yahoo.com,
clcarrion@tourism.gov.ph

Subic

Subic Bay Freeport Zone, SBMA, Olongapo City
☎ 047-252 7052, evening 047-252 5211
Contact: Randy Delara

Evacuation Assistance

AFP Search and Rescue Facilities GHQ, Philippine Air Force Villamor Airbase, Pasay City
☎ 02-911 6385

Avoid jellyfish stings

Urchin spines can be painful but wounds are easily treated

Luzon Dive Sites

Luzon is likely the first island you'll visit in the Philippines as it's where the capital and air hub, Manila, is found. Manila Bay has great sunsets but is quite polluted so divers usually head out pretty quickly to clearer skies and fresh air. But the city is still of use to divers as there are many dive centers that sell and fix gear, arrange trips and book live-aboards. And Luzon is the largest of the more than 7000 isles in the archipelago.

So once out of the big city, there are still plenty of destinations to see around the huge island. Old-time favorites in San Fernanado province are La Union, Subic Bay and its wrecks, and Anilao for reefs and macro. The relative newcomer is Bicol, which features Donsol and its mantas and whale sharks.

LA UNION

There are certainly plenty of sandy stretches named 'Long Beach' in Asia, and the 2-mile-long beach at San Fer-

nando is the Philippines' entry to this list. While still recovering from indiscriminate blast fishing in the not-too-distant past, the reef has its highlights. A lot of dive training takes place here because conditions favor year-round diving. It's only a five-hour drive out of Manila or a short plane-hop so it's a very popular weekend spot for training and groups.

While many of the better Philippine sites are seasonal, this area sits north of the typhoon belt and has protection

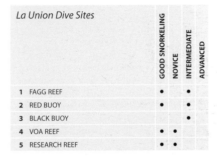

La Union Dive Sites	GOOD SNORKELING	NOVICE	INTERMEDIATE	ADVANCED
1 FAGG REEF	•		•	
2 RED BUOY	•		•	
3 BLACK BUOY			•	
4 VOA REEF	•	•		
5 RESEARCH REEF	•	•		

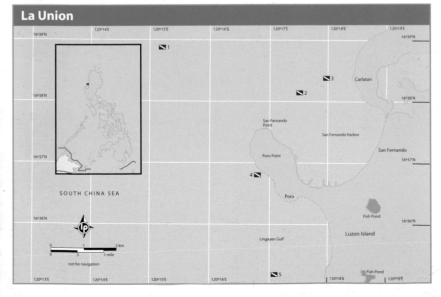

La Union

SOUTH CHINA SEA

not for navigation

San Fernando Point
San Fernando Harbor
San Fernando
Carlatan
Poro Point
Poro
Fish Pond
Luzon Island
Lingayen Gulf
Fish Pond

from the prevailing winds of the Lingayen Gulf. During peak season (March to June), visibility is excellent. Rainy-season visibility isn't terrible but may be around 30ft. Most diving is still done off the outrigger converted fishing bangkas but some shops are getting purpose-built fiberglass dive boats.

1 FAGG REEF

Location: *2 miles (3km) offshore of San Fernando*
Depth: *13-140ft (4-40m)*
Access: *Boat*
Range: *Intermediate*

On this large reef, a massive wall slopes down to the extremely deep continental shelf, which skirts the shore before sweeping west around Cape Bolinao across the Lingayen Gulf. The reef top has some interesting bommies (bombora), as well as sandy lanes that run

Bigeye jacks flow over the reef

between rocky outcrops covered in a variety of hard and soft corals. The assortment of large fish and other sea creatures includes king barracuda, rays, Napoleon wrasses, dogtooth tuna, jacks, turtles, mackerel and wahoos and even the possibility of a marlin.

Whale sharks have been seen cruising off the wall by divers making a safety swap (after having been swept off the reef).

Perhaps the most interesting attractions on Fagg Reef are the M10A1E tanks. At the end of WWII, US forces scrapped these tanks and dropped them off a barge. Luckily for divers, three came to rest on a small ledge 131ft to 144ft off Fagg's west wall. Although on the very edge of achievable for recreational scuba divers (you have about three minutes' bottom time before you need to ascend to off-gas on the shallower reef sections), these are excellent technical diving sites. Two other tanks lie deeper and are definitely tech dives.

2 RED BUOY

Location: *San Fernando Harbor*
Depth: *10-125ft (3-38m)*
Access: *Boat*
Range: *Intermediate and/or with guide*

At times there actually is a red buoy to mark this site, although storms may wash it away during the rainy season as the harbor mouth is quite exposed. A strong current sometimes washes out of the harbor, attracting pelagics such as dogtooth tuna, mackerel, jacks and, very occasionally, some sharks and leopard rays.

A short wall drops from 18ft to 100ft. Southwest of the wall the reef is quite shallow and largely bombed out, but some pronounced ravines and crevices

Safety Sausage a Must

A safety sausage is a vertical float that is deployed while you are underwater on your safety stop. If you deploy it at a dive's end, the dive boat can see you if you are drifting with the currents. In the Philippines, normally your guide would do this. But if you get separated, use your sausage. It's important.

The Philippines is one place you really want to have a safety sausage. The healthy, diverse reefs here are in great shape because they are constantly being flushed and fed by currents. Now remember, currents are our friends. Without them, the sea life would go elsewhere. If you want to see the best reefs and most interesting marine life, you will have to dive where there are some moderate to strong currents. A safety sausage will help you avoid harmful contact with the reefs.

Another reason to have a safety sausage is that boat traffic in the Philippines can be horrendous in the popular dive and snorkel spots. Dive bubbles can't be seen at times or aren't paid attention to. Your head could easily become part of some fisherman's or snorkel charter boat's propeller. Always carry your own safety sausage and use it, and/or always go up very close to your guide and let him or her go up first. It's their job to watch out for your topknot.

A divemaster releases a safety sausage

provide shelter for the large fish that find their way into them.

About 650ft away, so a bit of a swim from the wall, is an impressive depression known as the **Fishbowl**. It looks like a large amphitheater. Although the reef lacks many healthy corals, the Fishbowl's great visibility attracts lots of fish. Pelagics seem to like swimming around the bowl's circumference looking for a snack, which could include groupers, snappers, parrotfish, wrasses, blennies, squirrelfish or any one of the number of other smaller species that divers often see here.

| 3 | **BLACK BUOY** |

Location: *San Fernando Harbor*
Depth: *10-100ft (3-30m)*
Access: *Boat*
Range: *Intermediate*

OK, so there really isn't a black buoy here, but years (two or more decades) ago one marked the channel into the harbor, and the name has been used ever since. Most *banceros* can find the site easily enough – it's just south of where the reef breaks the surface at low tide.

Visibility can be quite poor, as the water is usually turbid. When the tide ebbs and flows from the nearby muddy harbor, a lot of sediment washes over the broken-up reef top, but there usually isn't much of a current once you start down the precipitous wall.

The deeper section of the wall is pocked by more than 20 caves. These are known to be home to big lobsters. Some may shelter sleeping whitetips and, occasionally, nurse sharks.

You really don't have to dive any deeper than 50ft here and there are some nice coral heads in the area plus big cracks and crevices.

4	VOA REEF

Location: *Off Poro Point*
Depth: *13-120ft (4-36m)*
Access: *Boat*
Range: *All levels*

VOA (Voice of America) Reef, named for the US radio station's massive antenna that dominates the Poro Point Peninsula, is another good training and night-dive site and an excellent snorkeling area. The reef starts right at the shore and runs out more than 1000ft. It tops out at 13ft and reaches down to 75ft. Unlike at Long Beach, the sea bottom here is covered in coral sand. The visibility tends to be better because coral sand, which is heavier than the sediment prevalent at many sites, sinks rapidly back to the bottom after turbulence.

The inshore side of the reef has lots of sandy areas with healthy coral bommies growing all over the place. Brain, table and boulder corals and a few basket sponges predominate. The sand is dotted with many anemones, some sea

whips and lots of shells (including green turbans, several species of cowries, augers and cone shells).

The seaward reef wall is also quite good, with a few gorgonians and plenty of hard corals, as well as some really bright, orange and red soft corals at the southern end, which is a good 35ft deeper than the northern end.

5	RESEARCH REEF

Location: *Off Long Beach, Buang*
Depth: *7-92ft (2-28m)*
Access: *Boat*
Range: *Novice/Intermediate*

Research Reef has many sites worth visiting along the shallower beach side and also along the deeper, small wall on its seaward side. The reef top is at about 18ft, and the reef slopes to a sandy bottom at about 92ft deep.

From shore you can swim out to some pretty coral gardens between 7ft to 35ft deep that are good for training dives and snorkeling. The seafloor is a mixture of sand and silt dotted with coral bommies all the way out to the reef.

The most popular area of Research Reef is the **Caves**, where several small cave-like passageways cut through the reef – even novice divers can swim through these. The largest passage is on the reef's west face. Lobsters are usually seen here, especially at night. There are also some shrimp-clogged cleaning stations sheltered in these caves.

From here a knowledgeable dive guide can take you over the sandy bottom to some large coral bommies that rise to within 30ft of the surface. One of these has a 65ft passageway going into its center. The entrance is at 80ft.

Hawksbill turtles were once common in this area, but fewer are seen these

One-stripe anemonefish in a sea anemone

days. Fish life is quite varied, including small groupers, jacks, snappers, sweetlips, parrotfish, many anemones with clownfish, a few leatherjackets and some octopuses. Lots of smaller reef fish and fry dart about between the few healthy hard and soft corals and the skeletons of the reef's former glory.

Blue-spotted rays and lots of map and tiger cowries rest in the sand. Occasionally you might catch a glimpse of a pelagic or two, especially away from the wall, where the visibility often drops considerably. Research is also a good night-diving spot, shallow and full of marine life, albeit mostly smaller fish.

SUBIC BAY

Olongapo, on Subic Bay, is closer to Manila than La Union. It's a 2½- to 3½-hour drive northwest of metro Manila. You can also take a 20-minute flight from Manila. The former US naval base at Olongapo is now a free port (duty-free) zone with a number of relatively pricey hotels on offer. Nearby you'll find several fair beaches with basic infrastructure, as well as accommodations ranging from modest to quite luxurious.

Wreck diving is the order of the day. And most of Subic Bay's best diving is in the harbor. Of varying antiquity

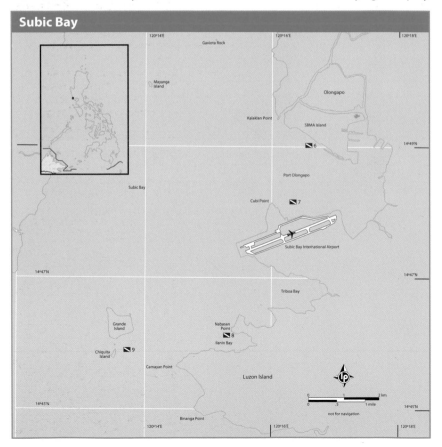

and structural integrity, the sunken hulks hail from as far back as the Spanish–American War of 1898, WWI and WWII. The WWII wrecks are mostly Japanese and are the result of US air attacks that occured during the retaking of the country.

Visibility can be elusive. Again the best weather is usually between January and June.

If wrecks aren't your thing, Grande Island is a good site for both divers and for snorkelers to explore. You can also arrange trips to the Capones Islands, a couple of hours north of Subic, through a couple of local dive centers.

Subic also has a fully functional recompression chamber staffed by experienced professionals. You are welcome to visit and tour the facility, but try to do so as a guest, not as a customer.

Subic Bay	GOOD SNORKELING	NOVICE	INTERMEDIATE	ADVANCED
6 ORYOKU MARU				•
7 USS NEW YORK				•
8 EL CAPITAN				•
9 SAN QUENTIN				•

6 ORYOKU MARU

Location: *0.5km off Alava Pier*
Depth: *50-65ft (15-20m)*
Access: *Boat*
Range: *Intermediate*

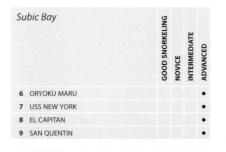

Divers like this wreck for its bloody history. Following a US air attack during WWII, it was discovered that more than 1600 US prisoners of war were onboard Japanese vessels, all of whom perished in the attack. 'Hellship' was the name given to unmarked Japanese freighters that had allied POWs onboard. Allied forces would attack not knowing they were incidentally attacking their countrymen. Three hundred men died on this particular ship.

After the war, the wreck was flattened by the US navy, as it lay in a major shipping channel. As a consequence, it is not the best wreck dive but it is an interesting tangle of mangle.

Not much is left to suggest the wreck was once a Japanese passenger vessel, but it's now home to a variety of fish, including a resident shoal of barracuda, sweetlips, fusiliers, angelfish,

Schooling blackbar barracuda

butterfly fish, triggerfish and many others.

Soft corals and some hard corals, sponges and hydroids cover much of the remaining superstructure, and you may be lucky enough to spot a lobster or two in the debris. The current can pick up here, and the visibility, which can vary from 10ft to 50ft is usually better just after high tide.

7 | USS NEW YORK

Location: *15 minutes by boat from Alava Pier*
Depth: *50-92ft (15-28m)*
Access: *Boat*
Range: *Advanced with guide*

This dive on a US battleship is the most impressive wreck site in Subic Bay. Commissioned in 1899 as the USS *Rochester* and subsequently renamed *Saratoga* and then *New York*, this vessel saw action in Manila Bay during the Spanish–American War, in China during the Chinese Revolution (also

A resident lionfish

Wreck-Diving Safety

Wreck diving can be fascinating, and safe if you take the proper precautions. Penetration of shipwrecks is a skilled specialty and should not be attempted without proper training. Wrecks are often unstable; they can be silty, deep and disorienting. Use an experienced guide to view wrecks and the amazing coral communities that have developed on them. Make sure all of your gear is tucked in if you attempt even a minor penetration and keep fin movement to an absolute minimum. A good wreck-dive training course is well worth the investment to enhance both the comfort and safety of the experience.

known as the War of Liberation) and throughout the Pacific during WWI. Decommissioned in 1932, she was stripped of most of her fittings and lay at anchor for 10 years off the Alava Pier before retreating US forces scuttled her to prevent the guns from falling into the hands of the advancing Japanese army.

She now rests on her port side in 92ft, relatively intact save for the enormous holes from the scuttling demolition. The bow of the *New York* is distinctive, as it slopes forward rather than astern from the deck. Many gun ports are mounted along the sides of the vessel. It is one of only a few diveable battleships in the world and certainly the shallowest of such wrecks.

The most prominent features of this wreck are of course the guns, but the battleship is easily penetrable. Most of the potential diver hazards were removed during her decommissioning. Make sure you have an experienced guide and are qualified to penetrate a wreck, as the vessel is massive, and it's easy to get lost in the maze of corridors and passageways.

Diver inside a hold with lionfish

The *New York* is now liberally festooned with sponges, hydroids and a variety of soft corals. Watch out for the many lionfish. Other fish life includes some large triggerfish, sweetlips, fusiliers and batfish. Look inside the main interior passageway for a colony of groupers. A few spiny lobsters still survive in the many nooks and crannies. On deck, you may find yourself encircled by an impressive shoal of barracuda cruising around the wreck. Divers sometimes see blue-spotted rays, especially along the muddy bottom of the bay.

Visibility on the wreck varies from approximately 10ft to 50ft. Diving at neap tide usually provides a chance for better visibility and great photo opportunities. Currents within the bay are usually negligible. Nearby are two Japanese shipwrecks, the *Oryoku Maru* and *Seian Maru*, that were sunk by US planes.

8	EL CAPITAN

Location: *Ilanin Bay*
Depth: *16-65ft (5-20m)*
Access: *Boat*
Range: *Advanced*

This is a great wreck dive that many repeat again and again. The attraction? Regarded by many as one of the best wreck dives in the Philippines, *El Capitan* is certainly one of the better wrecks for photography. Visibility, as with most sites in Subic Bay, ranges from 16ft to 50ft. Try to hit it just after high tide for the best chance at good visibility, and watch out for currents.

You come upon the wreck in only 16ft of water and, despite some serious

Scorpionfish can be found on many of the shipwrecks

damage to the vessel's structure, will immediately recognize this as a small freighter (425ft long, 3000 tons). This penetrable wreck lies on its port side with the bow at 65ft. It's covered in razor clams, lots of soft corals and sponges, hydroids and clouds of small tropical fish.

Some hard coral is dotted about the surrounding seafloor. Around the wreck resides a wide assortment of tropical fish, including lionfish, glasseyes, wrasses, tangs, gobies, batfish, damselfish, spotted sweetlips, crabs, clownfish and the occasional lobster.

But what is most photogenic about the ship on sunny days are the light shafts that stream through many places in the hull. The light dances and makes for both good stills and video.

9	SAN QUENTIN

Location: *Near Grande Island*
Depth: *40-53ft (12-16m)*
Access: *Boat*
Range: *Intermediate*

This is a chance to dive into the relics of a very different war. The Spanish scuttled the *San Quentin* in 1898 at the mouth of the bay to obstruct American warships. The wreck is mostly rubble but the bow and some of the steam boilers are still identifiable. It's surrounded by a variety of marine life, much of it larger than you will find within the bay itself. Look for wrasses, gobies, a shoal of glasseyes, tangs, spotted sweetlips, lobsters and crabs.

Close to the bay mouth, currents can be demanding at tide change so plan your dive carefully to avoid getting swept off the wreck into open water and away from the dive boat. As the site is somewhat exposed, the sea conditions can pick up quite quickly, making this a potentially uncomfortable ride to a rough entry and exit. However, because of the currents, visibility tends to be better here than in the bay.

ANILAO

Just south of Manila is Batangas province with some of the best marine-life diversity in the Philippines. This place is very popular on the weekends with

Anilao

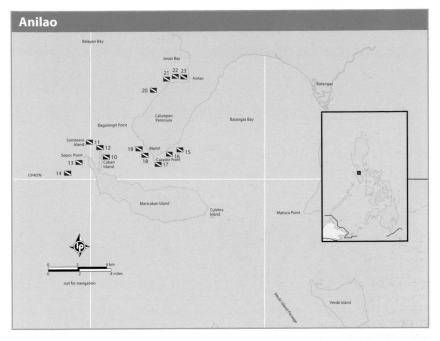

divers as it's only a couple of hours drive from Manila. Traffic can be forgiving and you can make the trip quickly on mostly good tollway road. Be warned though, on the way back if you're heading into Manila, traffic can be gridlocked, so give yourself plenty (repeat: plenty) of time if you have to catch a plane.

Once you get into the Balayan Bay area, the tiny port village of Anilao appears. From here, you continue on to the steep, hilly and lush terrain that is dotted with weekend retreats, dive centers and resorts. This is considered the birthplace of Philippine diving and there are well over 60 sites in the area from Janao Bay, around Bagalangit Point, to the Maricaban Island area and spilling into Batangas Bay. There are some showcase marine preserves full of fish, sea turtles and big jack schools. And Anilao is famous for its macro and muck diving, where it seems one odd critter after another pops up.

The surrounding area is rugged and very scenic. You may find getting to your resort requires a bit of a hike downhill. As a result, there aren't a lot of independent restaurants around even though the place is usually busy with weekend

Anilao Dive Sites	GOOD SNORKELING	NOVICE	INTERMEDIATE	ADVANCED
10 KIRBY'S ROCK	•	•		
11 SOMBRERO ISLAND	•		•	
12 BAJURA	•		•	
13 SEPOK WALL	•		•	
14 MAPATING	•		•	
15 SPRING BUBBLES			•	
16 SECRET BAY	•		•	
17 MAINIT	•		•	
18 TWIN ROCKS	•	•		
19 ELMER'S			•	
20 CATHEDRAL ROCK	•		•	
21 OUTRIGGER HOUSE REEF	•		•	
22 BASURA 1			•	
23 BASURA 2				•

Anthias are thick at Kirby's Rock

revelers and beachgoers. But the hillside and beach locations are open to gentle sea breezes and most face the western sunset.

While the weekends are big here, during the week when everyone heads back to Manila, some operations may be run by a skeleton crew. Thus, you may be able to swing some cash-saving midweek deals. Just make sure the dive staff knows you're coming so there's a boat, guide (and chef) for you. These midweek trips are nice as you usually find the dive sites less crowded and can even have them all to yourself. You can also get more personalized dive training this way.

There are a number of marine sanctuaries in the area and the trend is growing to add more.

10 KIRBY'S ROCK

Location: *North of Maricaban Island's western point*
Depth: *10-130ft (3-42m)*
Access: *Boat*
Range: *Advanced*

You may see a few different spellings of this site (Kirby's, Kerbis etc) but it's all the same place and it is a nice combination of deep and shallow. This is like two dives in one with a deep seamount full of life and then a mini wall and shallow pinnacle a bit further on in the dive. You don't have to go to the deepest part of the dive to see the beautiful sunken mounts or rock. The top of it is at 65ft but the sand below is at 125ft or so.

Divers enter the water at a buoy shrouded by the high cliffline of the elongated Maricaban Island and normally head straight down to the deepest part of the dive that is a stunning sunken pinnacle at 65ft to 100ft. Healthy corals, plenty of anthias and shoaling fusiliers highlight this deep oasis of life. Be careful of the strong currents that sometimes roll over the area. But you can usually hide on one side, away from the current, if it's bothersome.

Then head back up to the mini wall starting at 70ft, keeping the reef on the left. Here you will find plenty of nudibranchs, hiding spiny lionfish and small, brilliant-yellow sea cucumbers.

As the dive ends, head into the shallows where the pinnacle pokes out of the water. Between the pinnacle and the Maricaban cliffs, there's a crack or crevasse full of sea life and more of the colorful anthias. Look also for juvenile batfish and lots of silvery baitfish. This ball of movement forms a cloud in 10ft to 15ft of water. It makes for good entertainment and photo subjects as you decompress (deco) from the multifaceted dive.

11	SOMBRERO ISLAND

Location: *North of Maricaban Island's western point*
Depth: *20-90ft (6-27m)*
Access: *Boat*
Range: *Advanced*

Sombrero looks exactly like its namesake. Bangkas like to pull up to the white-sand beach where divers can get off, have a deco stop and eat lunch. Explore the beach and snorkel the shallows and the rocks here to see some nice table corals and an occasional sea turtle.

The island has some impressive drop-offs that further enhance its similarity to the broad-brimmed hat. It's home to some great diving as well, most notably at adjacent Beatrice Rock.

Crevices, tunnels and piles of large boulders are scattered off Sombrero Island's northern cliffs, and the drop-off delves to 88ft on the island's western side.

Be sure to follow the guide as currents are usually strong here. Divers can expect some pelagic action, most notably rainbow runners and yellowtails. There are some beautiful staghorn coral gardens and lots of bright yellow crinoids at shallower depths. Divers sometimes see a few species of larger rays, including the odd eagle ray. The reef itself is festooned with gorgonians, black coral, shells and lots of soft corals. Grunts, jacks, snappers and, if you're lucky, hawksbill turtles are common visitors here. As at Cathedral Rock, a small Catholic shrine was placed here at around 43ft.

Purpletip anemone with an ocellaris clownfish

Tomato clownfish, anemones, crinoids and other sea life can be found at Bajura and Sepok

A flowing marine worm

12 | BAJURA

Location: *Maricaban's north point*
Depth: *40-121ft (12-37m)*
Access: *Boat*
Range: *Advanced*

Bajura reef, just off the northern point of Maricaban Island, is more than half a mile long. It's a challenging snorkeling site because of the strong currents and often-rough sea conditions. But when it's calm, snorkelers will share the area with fishermen who move in for a chance to catch something from their small outriggers.

Bajura's fish life is similar to Sombrero's but more prolific. Lots of caves and overhangs provide resting places for whitetip sharks, and the reef is also home to parrotfish, butterflyfish, wrasses, lionfish, sweetlips, snappers, scorpionfish, surgeonfish, angelfish, batfish and an occasional eagle ray, among others.

The current is usually strong here, which keeps the coral vibrant and healthy. These include table, staghorn and smaller mushroom corals, as well as a lot of soft corals and crinoids. Follow the guide to avoid any pitfalls the current may present and you'll have a rewarding dive in this diverse site.

13 | SEPOK WALL

Location: *Westernmost point of Maricaban Island*
Depth: *14-100ft (4.5-30m)*
Access: *Boat*
Range: *Intermediate*

Sepok Wall, also called Philip's Garden, covered in a variety of soft and hard corals, drops off impressively from west of Sepok Point to the southwest. This is a good place for macro photography, although there are opportunities for wide angle. But nudibranch lovers will find this site rewarding with many

Flamboyant cuttlefish

colorful members of the Chromodoris family making this site home.

The wall starts in between 35ft in the south and about 27ft further up and drops to sand and some corals at around 70ft. It does get its share of pelagics cruising by so it doesn't hurt to look off into the blue for the occasional dogtooth tuna or schooling yellowtail fusiliers. Turtles enjoy the sandy plain below the wall and there are small corals and nice coral-covered bommies to the north about halfway into the dive.

After the dive, take a cruise around Maricaban Island and a look at the fishing village and natural formations along the coast before you head back to the Calumpan Peninsula.

14	MAPATING

Location: *Off Maricaban Island's western point*
Depth: *55-140ft (18-45m)*
Access: *Boat*
Range: *Advanced*

This brings us to Mapating, another dive rounding Maricaban's western point. This is an open-ocean reef just southwest of Sepok Point and wall. Although deep and isolated, you can't really say it's teeming with marine life. But this dive does offer a nice selection of big and small as well as corals at the reef top and a wall that drops to deep sand and then keeps dropping. As the currents are sometimes strong and it requires an open-water descent, this is a site for experienced divers only and should not be done without a knowledgeable guide.

Divers often see an impressive parade of pelagics, including large rays, whitetips and other shark species. The shallower portions of the reef are festooned with nudibranchs going about their business surrounded by prolific soft coral and some hard corals. The wall, which starts at around 59ft, runs quite a distance. A ledge at 66ft is sometimes used by resting nurse and cat sharks. Expect to see schools of surgeonfish and snappers along the wall.

For qualified deep divers, the entrance to a massive cave lies between 141ft and 157ft. This used to be home to resting sharks but the local divemasters say they have been fished out. You may get to see some large marble rays. This is beyond sport diving limits, however, and should only be done with proper deep and technical dive training and equipment.

water merges into the cooler seawater, creating a naturally heated underwater pool.

Unlike similar dive sites around the world, here the water is pretty hot where it bubbles from the seafloor, as is the surrounding sand. So feel the warmth and enjoy this oddity, but do it with care (and perhaps with gloves).

The reef top slopes down to an area that promises anything from sea anemones to sea snakes at the 40ft to 50ft area. From there you can drop over the edge of a small wall that is home to nudibranchs and the occasional big female yellow frogfish. The sandy area at the wall's bottom and toward the north attracts whitetip sharks and bluespot and marble rays, among others. Because of the unique underwater environment, the visibility is almost always good here.

A further bonus is that you can prepare lunch while diving. We said it was hot: at the start of your dive simply place an egg over one of the hot-water vents. You will find it quite hard-boiled and ready to eat by the time you finish your dive. Bring some salt and pepper.

15 | SPRING BUBBLES

Location: *S-SW of Sepok Wall*
Depth: *10-130ft (3-40m)*
Access: *Boat*
Range: *Novice/Intermediate*

A fascinating and unusual dive site, Spring Bubbles' main feature is, you guessed it, volcanic bubbles. Here, hot springs from beneath the sea create bubbles that flow up to the surface. At 33ft at the north end of the site, volcanically heated fresh water gushes from cracks in the seafloor. The area is covered in unusual bright green, yellow and pastel-hued soft corals. The hot

Blue damsels hover around a crinoid

16 SECRET BAY

Location: *Maricaban Island*
Depth: *9-100ft (3-25m)*
Access: *Shore & Boat*
Range: *Novice*

A seahorse on a sea pen

This pleasant sandy slope also features a few hot-water vents down deep and some oddly colored hot-springs-tainted sand that attracts a great variety of macro creatures. There is one hotel along the beach here and not much else, so boat traffic is light, making this the kind of dive that you can start deep and work your way up the slope to the shallows for a nice, long mucky session.

Photography conditions are quite nice with the bottom sandy but not too silty. There's a current that sweeps away your fin wash or your buddy's, so photos don't suffer from too much scatter if you just wait a minute. Sand anemones, Halimeda algae that hides small invertebrates and sea pens sprout from the seafloor. There's a bit of debris here and there and you may find an octopus or seahorse attached.

Other oddities include fire urchins, fluorescent urchins, feather worms, lots of gobies and their bulldozer shrimp, tiny stonefish, mantis shrimp and hermit crabs. It's a great macro spot that also has some very photogenic bobtail shrimp on the sand anemones. And look underneath the anemones for a hiding spotted crab.

17 MAINIT

Location: *Off Cazador Point*
Depth: *16-115ft (5-35m)*
Access: *Boat*
Range: *Intermediate*

This rocky point is one of the better dives for variety and fish life. *Mainit* means 'hot' in Tagalog and nearby onshore there are hot springs. You can bring eggs and boil them here too if you wish.

You see none of this underwater but you will see a good variety of terrain along a rocky, boulder-strewn, ridged and sloped reef. The dive starts in a protected eddy and, keeping the reef on the right, gets progressively better as you head into the currency point. There are lots of soft and hard corals including big clusters of salmon-colored *Tubastreas* that have bright-yellow polyps that feed when the current is strong.

There are stonefish and lots of lionfish about as well.

You may see a lot of small rocks with pieces of twine tied to them. This is a local fishing method and the rocks are the aftermath.

Look also for big, green tree *Tubastreas*, big plate and vase corals and lots of crinoids. There are many big, healthy barrel sponges along the drop-off as well. Although the rocky, sloping wall goes quite deep, the shallower areas hold much more to see so you can make a nice long dive between 40ft and 60ft just looking for small stuff such as nudibranchs and cowries.

At 90ft a small cave is occasionally graced by resting whitetip sharks, but this has become a rarity. There are also a couple of nearby submerged pinnacles at 70ft that offer a good vantage point from which to see the passing parade of pelagics when the current is running.

Heading back to the shallows, look for a host of sea anemones. There is one with beautiful purple tips and some resident ocellaris (like Nemo) clownfish that makes a great photo subject.

| 18 | **TWIN ROCKS** |

Location: *NW of Calzador Point*
Depth: *6-100ft (2-30m)*
Access: *Shore & Boat*
Range: *Novice*

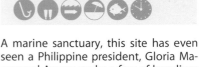

A marine sanctuary, this site has even seen a Philippine president, Gloria Macapagal Arroyo make a few of her dives here. The site only allows 20 divers at a time, according to a sign on the beach, and does not allow training or checkout. So the good news here is that you will have the place pretty much to yourself most of the time and only 19 other divers on the weekends.

The fish here are used to being fed so you may see batfish headed your way before you are even on the bottom. They are normally fed bread. And other fish such as damsels and butterflyfish will join the fray. The dive is started at the south buoy and divers can feed the fish, look at the corals and check out sea anemones and even some well-placed

A hawksbill turtle in the Twin Rocks preserve

The beautiful Chromodoris bullocki nudibranch

giant clams. There are some Tridacnas near the remains of a wreck. Other wreck remnants sit at 100ft but aren't much to see, although they can house odd small critters.

Go a bit deeper down the sloping bottom and you may see a large school of bigeye jacks. The fish seem to have an uncanny sense of the sanctuary, as do the sea turtles; they all stay right within its borders. Look for hawksbills resting on the bottom including an occasional big, old male.

Toward the end of the dive 'the twins' appear in the shallows. They are two similar-looking rocks split by a small canyon in the middle. They are shallow and smothered in marine life. If you've been diving deeper, take care not to break your deco here by coming too shallow on the shore side. Pink anthias are everywhere. Yellow and orange crinoids nestle on balls of the pink *Tubastreas*. If there is some current, the *Tubastreas* open their yellow polyps giving the twins even more color. Anemones and all kinds of hard corals cover the rest of the rocks.

End the dive by looking at the fish life and hard corals. There is a large stand of fluorescent green coral that would look quite cool under a night black light.

19 | ELMER'S

Location: *NW of, almost adjacent to, Twin Rocks*
Depth: *15-100ft (4-30m)*
Access: *Boat*
Range: *Novice*

This is a great macro site almost adjacent to the Twin Rocks Marine Sanctuary and it is good for sea anemones, corals and a variety of nudibranchs including quite a few from the Nembrotha family. The majority of these can be seen in the 25ft

to 60ft range and the site is very good for macro photography.

A bonus is that this area isn't dived much as it's known as a site that 'only photographers enjoy'. The reason they like it for the colorful oddities such as flamboyant cuttlefish, pygmy seahorses, Spanish dancers, the beautiful purple *Chromodoris (Hypselodoris bullocki)*.

There are also some attractive plume worms, the occasional blue ribbon eel and lots of anemones throughout the dive including bubble tip anemones with spinecheek clownfish. Photographers do love the place but anybody into small and odd will enjoy this dive.

20 | CATHEDRAL ROCK

Location: *NE of Babalangit Point*
Depth: *30-100ft (9-30m)*
Access: *Shore & Boat*
Range: *Novice*

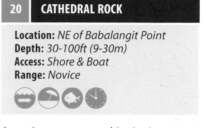

A marine sanctuary, this site is a popular weekend haunt for Manila divers. Nudibranch lovers flock here for macro photography.

White-eyed moray

A colorful Chromodoris nudibranch

There are a few other sites around the country named the same thing, but this Cathedral Rock site is, without a doubt, the most famous. It's actually a flourishing artificial reef developed in 1967 by scuba enthusiast Dr Tim Sevilla. This diving pioneer transplanted the now-prodigious live corals onto the previously barren twin rocks. Before Sevilla, this was an act thought to be impossible. These rocks are now teeming with fish awaiting a handout from divers, who for years have been feeding them. The success of this ground-breaking project has spurred a few other endeavors, such as the thriving artificial reef in the making at the end of Basura 1.

This is also one of a handful of sites in the area that are both protected and allow fish feeding. This makes getting fish photos pretty easy. Just don't throw out too much food at once or you'll have a frenzy of damsels, surgeons and batfish on your hands.

At around 48ft you'll notice the small cross from which the site gets its name. The cross was blessed by Pope John Paul II and placed here in 1983 by then-General Fidel V Ramos, who went on to become president of the Philippines.

It is possible to go deeper than 98ft, but there isn't much to see below the Cathedral's localized action, which typically includes nudibranchs, Moorish idols, butterflyfish, clownfish hanging around some copious anemones, angelfish, triggerfish, wrasses, parrotfish, damsels, puffers, surgeons and even juvenile batfish in the shallows.

21 | OUTRIGGER HOUSE REEF

Location: *Matutunggil Rock*
Depth: *15-100ft (16-30m)*
Access: *Shore & Boat*
Range: *Novice/Intermediate*

This site is being developed by the Scuba World dive staff at the nearby Anilao Outrigger as its house reef and it is taking pains to try to keep it from being fished for the benefit of divers and snorkelers. It's not an official marine park but the staff is working to see it treated as such.

At the rocky point where the Outrigger sits, Matutunggil Rock, there's a white-sand shelf. This spills down into a protected bay that is good for both day and night dives. Boat traffic is low unless you venture too far out around the corner.

There have been a couple of giant clams transplanted here, which are fun to see. They feed from the sun (using the little black dots on their mantle to synthesize the energy to feed plants in their tissue) and if a diver passes over them, they will try to close. But the big Tridacnas have such large mantles, they really can't close all the way.

Look for small anemones and coral heads. The guides have their favorite critter haunts and can show them to you. Afterwards, you can return for easy shore dives on your own once you're familiar with the layout. After a dive day, it's great to watch the sun set over Matutunggil Rock.

Razorfish hovering

22 | BASURA 1

Location: *South coast Balayan Bay*
Depth: *10-80ft (3-25m)*
Access: *Shore & Boat*
Range: *Novice*

This was once the most famous critter dive in Anilao. A typhoon in 2006 altered the make-up of things and the site since hasn't really returned to prominence as far as sheer variety of strange muck creatures goes. However, it is still very rewarding. Some divers say night

Muck Diving

The term 'muck diving' is attributed to Papua New Guinea dive pioneer Bob Halstead. He found that there were unusual, exotic and juvenile critters near his wife's home at Dinah's Beach at Milne Bay. These odd and unusual creatures make their homes in the volcanic black sand, sediment and even trash that the popular sites and bays seem to have in common. Lucky divers may find colorful nudibranchs, frogfish, blue-ringed octopuses, scorpionfish, seahorses and a host of other strange and hard-to-find marine creatures in these habitats. While not as pretty as coral reefs, muck dives are fascinating and require a sharp eye and knowledge of how a fish or invertebrate uses camouflage. Perhaps those that enjoy muck diving the most are the macro photographers. The normally calm and shallow water provides amazing opportunities to photograph the creatures and the dives are normally longer, providing plenty of bottom time. Anilao Is considered one of the better muck diving regions in the Philippines.

A tiny octopus hides in a broken bottle

diving here is best – a few even go to the extreme of sleeping by day and making two or three dives here at night. Others think the site is good any time of the day. Photographer Scott 'Gutsy' Tuason produced a very nice hard cover book called *Anilao* that features a lot of Basura's macro critters.

Basura means 'trash' in Tagalog and you will see that the prevailing currents seem to carry junk here and leave it. But this trash is quickly converted into habitat by octopuses, seahorses, frogfish and scorpionfish.

There are also a lot of naturally occurring sand anemones with clownfish, crabs and shrimp. Look for fluorescent corals and a brilliant fluoro red sea anemone at the start of the dive. Other critters include nudibranchs, various pipefish, small eels and mantis shrimp.

At the end of the dive is a home-made coral garden that owners of a nearby dive resort have planted in hopes of someday creating a reef. It's very pretty and dreamlike, and hides small puffers and razorfish.

23	BASURA 2

Location: *South coast Balayan Bay*
Depth: *10-80ft (3-25m)*
Access: *Shore & Boat*
Range: *Novice*

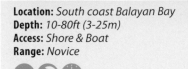

This site is a continuation of the first dive and extends almost into Anilao town. The terrain isn't as sandy. It's scattered with more coral bommies and holds a different host of small fish. It's known to be a very good place to find ribbon eels, but there are also a lot of nudibranchs, including hammerhead nudis.

Look for striped fantail pipefish in the urchins, cardinalfish schools, plumeworms, and plenty of guardian sand gobies with their bulldozer shrimp. There are also many roaming shoals of juvenile catfish scouring the bottom. This can be another long and shallow dive.

LEGASPI/DONSOL

Most folks get to Donsol by flying in to southern Luzon via Legaspi. This area has what has been described as the perfect volcano. The imposing Mt Mayon looms over Legaspi City and the surrounding countryside. Since the airport is a bit out of town, you can miss city traffic and take the hour-long ride through the surrounding countryside into the province of Sorosogon. There are many scenic overlooks and opportunities for volcano snaps along the way.

After about 30 minutes, the road to Donsol turns off from the main road and is a fun zigzag affair that rolls through beautiful rice paddies reminiscent of rural Bali. There are also some great photo ops along this stretch.

A 25-minute ride brings you to the riverfront town of Donsol. Some divers and whale sharkers stay in town where there are some trendy restaurants and a good night market. Most stay at the resorts a few miles out of town along the beach where there are also some very good little eateries. Make sure you try the Bicol Express at Amor Farm Beach Resort. It is a spicy local dish and a real taste treat. The Barracuda has some superb butterfly prawns and the Vitton Beach Resort next to the local Department of Tourism station has a great selection of adobo and Filipino food. The fiesta for the town is in late May and is good fun with a beer garden, lots of food and games.

To see the whale sharks, everyone must get a license and take a course that is run by the Department of Tourism – it's on video and is well done and entertaining. World Wildlife Fund guidelines for whale shark interaction are generally followed in Donsol waters.

The best time to visit is October to June as the north monsoon, 'habagat' in Bikol language, blows in from July to September and makes water rough and creates low visibility in the bay. Manta Bowl escapes this low bay visibility but it can be a rough ride out and also difficult for the boat to find you at the end of the dive in the high seas.

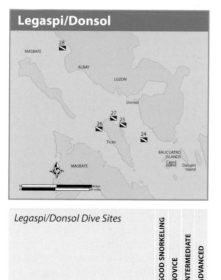

The Mayon volcano can be seen over Donsol Bay

Legaspi/Donsol Dive Sites	GOOD SNORKELING	NOVICE	INTERMEDIATE	ADVANCED
24 MANTA BOWL	•	•		
25 BOBBY'S WALL	•		•	
26 BOBBY'S GARDEN	•		•	
27 ALEA BEACH	•		•	
28 SAN RAFAEL	•		•	

A manta at Manta Bowl

24 MANTA BOWL

Location: *Ticao Island channel*
Depth: *55-80ft (17-25m)*
Access: *Boat*
Range: *Advanced*

This is one of the major pelagic dive sites in the Philippines and is normally current swept and full of a variety of open-water marine life. But don't let the current deter you. Divers bring reef hooks, hook in and wait for the large creatures to show up. This is a tricky dive, however, and should be done only with an experienced guide.

From Donsol, it's about an hour ride in calm seas to the dive area. There are no moorings and an open water fast descent is required to get to the reef top. Since the reef is only 55ft to 60ft in many spots, this is done fairly easily.

Donsol guides say the currents average two to four knots and visibility is best at high morning tide. Stick close to the guide and be weighted enough to avoid being swept away. You will find the top of the mount has some low scattered coral heads but most of it is open. These coral stations usually hold sea anemones with clownfish, lots of crinoids and a few other small fish such as hawkfish and chromis.

There are cleaning stations along the reef top of this broad seamount in the Ticao Straits. They are not obvious, but a good guide will show you where to hook in and observe. Also, some of the better spots are bit deeper at 80ft as the reef top slopes gradually down in the direction of the current flow.

Among the many big fish you can expect to see here are, of course, marble rays, big oceanic mantas, tiger sharks, oceanic whitetips, great hammerhead sharks and whale sharks. Local guide Bobby Adrao has done more than 1500 dives here since it was first pioneered in 1998. He says it's not unusual to see both whale sharks (in season) and mantas at the same cleaning stations. His personal record for manta sightings was 32 rays on one dive.

The strong currents also bring out the schooling fish and it's common to see large great barracuda, blackbar barracuda shoals, schooling bigeye jacks and even yellowfin tuna.

Visibility can vary here and is best at high tide. Trips usually start early to take advantage of morning tide.

The fish life, especially the big fish, decreases significantly at slack tide. Low tide can also bring in the fish but visibility can be low as there is a large mangrove system on one side of the straits in massive Sorsogon Bay that empties into these straits.

After watching the action, unhook your reef hook and do an open-ocean drift deco stop, again following the guide and his safety sausage. Because this is really out to open sea and it has currents, each diver should have a safety sausage in case he or she gets swept off and is separated from the group or guide. The hardcore manta and big fish addicts do a three-dive day here.

There may be jellyfish at the deco stop level so take care to avoid any stings or stray tentacles from these ocean drifters. Bring along some vinegar just in case.

Fireflies

Some places in the Philippines offer evening natural-light shows and Donsol is one of them. The trees along the river adjacent to town attract tiny fireflies that have a powerful strobe. Their flashing light is due to a chemical reaction called bioluminescence. This process occurs in these little fireflies from a specialized light-emitting organ on the firefly's lower abdomen; an enzyme acts on luciferin and oxygen to produce light. The swarm of fireflies covers some trees, and the constant flashing makes the trees light up as if they are decorated for Christmas. Tropical fireflies routinely synchronize their flashes and the effect is like a coordinated light show.

Just after sunset, a boat can meet you on the beach at your resort and travel down the ocean shoreline near town where you will cross the delta, go under the town's new, single-lane bridge and head upriver where large trees and nipa palms line the river banks. Under a starry sky it's a great way to enjoy nature's free lightshow.

River fireflies

Banded sea snake

25 | BOBBY'S WALL

Location: *South point of San Miguel*
Depth: *30-100ft (9-30m)*
Access: *Boat*
Range: *Intermediate*

Along the west side and the far point of San Miguel island there is a drift dive along a wall that is fun and full of surprises. This is normally a drift dive with a manageable current running along the steep cliffs. These cliffs are nice to see above the surface as they hold caves and have splendid formations.

Below they also offer exploration as the diver can enter any one of three caves at about 70ft and look for inhabitants.

Inside and along the wall and sea bottom you can find boxer shrimp in the cave, banded sea snakes, stonefish, spotted stingrays and many kinds of nudibranchs.

The wall and caves also have colorful arrays of soft corals. Drift and then explore. This site is good for both macro and wide-angle photography.

26 | BOBBY'S GARDEN

Location: *South tip of San Miguel Island, east side*
Depth: *10-60ft (3-20m)*
Access: *Boat*
Range: *Novice*

Blue starfish can be seen while snorkeling at Bobby's Garden

Pufferfish in coral at Alea Beach

This is a relaxing and shallow boat dive that can be done on the way back from Manta Bowl or as a second dive after the nearby Bobby's Wall. Both were found by local guide Bobby Adrao. This is a very new site and it features lots of small coral heads, table corals and undercuts to explore.

The bonus is that this seems to be a manta ray area as well and an occasional manta ray is seen around the table corals at 35ft to 40ft. Also look for eagle rays swimming by.

The corals hold various anemones and spinecheek clownfish, spiny puffers, lots of variety in nudibranchs, shrimp, crabs and lots of other small critters. This can be a good macro dive but some use wide angle just in case an eagle ray or manta shows up.

27 ALEA BEACH

Location: *San Miguel Island, west side*
Depth: *0-10ft (0-3m)*
Access: *Boat or Beach*
Range: *Snorkel*

This is a private beach and permission to use it can be arranged in Donsol. But even if you don't go ashore, snorkeling from your anchored bangka is very nice. It's a shallow bay open on two sides and fairly protected from the wind and swell.

The bottom has small coral heads, brain corals and sea feathers. Lots of starfish are also found in the area. Look for pufferfish and lizardfish in the sea feathers and trumpetfish hiding in the fronds.

The site could be dived, but as the bay is fairly shallow throughout it's not really necessary.

28 SAN RAFAEL

Location: *Off San Rafael village, Donsol*
Depth: *5-30ft (1.2-9m)*
Access: *Boat*
Range: *Novice*

This is a shallow and mucky dive with just enough current to sweep the silt away, making photography rewarding despite silty conditions. Two is a crowd on this dive, as silt gets kicked up easily and visibility lessens quickly. Divers should spread out as there are lots of oddities all along the bottom.

Among the creatures seen here are hairy frogfish, waspfish, lots of saddleback anemonefish and their anemones with their aggressive little clownish, mantis shrimp, nudibranchs, small red or orange frogfish, fire urchins with zebra crabs and lots more.

It's in a fairly remote location and boat traffic is rare, but if you are up in the shallows, keep an ear out just in case. The ride back is scenic and you can see Mt Mayon on a clear day as the bangka motors along the shoreline off San Rafael.

Saddleback anemonefish in a sand anemone

Donsol's Whale Sharks

Young male Donsol whale shark

Whale sharks are the biggest species of shark and also the world's biggest fish. And Donsol's big claim to fame is that they show up annually and consistently in its waters to feed. They are here in the highest numbers from mid-February until the end of March but they can start to appear as early as late November or December if there have been no big rains. They leave in May when the hagabat winds start coming in and making the bay murky, and most of their food is gone.

The whale sharks that show up are young males, and not huge by whale shark standards, averaging 13ft to 20ft and 2 tons (whale sharks can reach 60ft, and average 40ft and 8 to 13 tons). However, Donsol's whale sharks are still bigger than anything else swimming around the bay. Thus, their dark forms can be seen cruising just under the surface in a tasty layer of Donsol Bay's plankton, small fish and crablets,

There is an association of whale-shark-watching boats and the crews are trained in spotting and approaching the sharks. The spotters have great eyes as the sharks rarely break the surface, and they can see the sharks even on overcast days without polarized glasses. Snorkelers are not allowed to touch the fish and everyone pays a fee that supports the conservation of the sharks.

The Department of Tourism, located right next to the Vitton Beach Resort about 8 miles out of town, issues permits and tries to follow WWF guidelines for whale-shark interaction. There was a count of 136 different whale sharks in 2008. When there are a lot of sharks around, it's a pretty civil affair with each boat achieving numerous chances for guests to see the sharks. Towards the start and end of the season it's a different story, with many boats trying to get their guests in the water with very few sharks. Try to go at the height of the season for the best shot at seeing multiple creatures in the smallest crowd. You can even charter your own boat for this.

Whale sharks have been good to Donsol. They were first offered as a protected attraction around 1997–98 and the resulting influx of tourist dollars has led to a new road, a new bridge and many new jobs from the resorts popping up for whale shark snorkeling and now for divers.

Mindoro Dive Sites

Looking out to sea from the Point

This rugged, mountainous island is one of the most popular, if not the most popular, destinations for divers visiting the Philippines. Most of the diving action is found off Sabang Bay and near Sabang.

The beaches and bays of the northeast tip of Mindoro Island are actually commonly referred to as Puerto Galera. Puerto Galera town is actually a bigger, nontourist city a bit southwest of Sabang. Generally, the whole area just gets called Puerto Galera but the divers mostly hang out around Sabang's beaches, which include Monkey Beach, Big La Laguna and Small La Laguna.

Mindoro Dive Sites	GOOD SNORKELING	NOVICE	INTERMEDIATE	ADVANCED
29 CLAM CITY		•	•	•
30 CORAL GARDENS	•	•	•	•
31 *ALMA JANE*		•	•	•
32 SABANG WRECKS		•	•	•
33 WEST ESCARCEO	•	•	•	•
34 HOLE IN THE WALL		•	•	•
35 THE CANYONS		•	•	•
36 SINADIGAN WALL		•	•	•
37 WASHING MACHINE			•	•
38 VERDE ISLAND WALL		•	•	•

Many expatriates from around the world call Puerto Galera home these days, drawn as much by the business opportunities it offers as by the wealth of natural assets it enjoys. Consequently, visitors will have no shortage of dining and entertainment options. Sabang, a commuter port city, is a mix of diver's haven and Kuta, Bali – lots of diving by day and lots of partying by night. Good local food stands line the beach, while fine dining can be found in the hotels. Accommodations are plentiful, ranging from simple beach cottages to air-conditioned resorts. The shoreline is the home of the famous Point Bar, where many dive stories are greatly embellished. World records for tequila consumption have been set here on New Year's Eves.

But food and revelry aside, there are dive shops that are very advanced and equipped well for anything from basic instruction all the way up to advanced tech. The Professional Association of Diving Instructors (PADI) is the predominant agency here, as it is throughout the country.

Puerto Galera is easily accessible. Folks who fly in usually take a two-hour bus ride from Manila to Batangas then a one-hour crossing of the Verde Island Passage. Most resorts and dive centers can arrange transfers from anywhere in Manila. Boat transfers to and from Anilao are also common and take anywhere from 40 minutes to two hours depending on the boat and the currents.

There's a perfect, natural harbor endowed with a stunningly beautiful

Schooling batfish are common in Puerto Galera waters

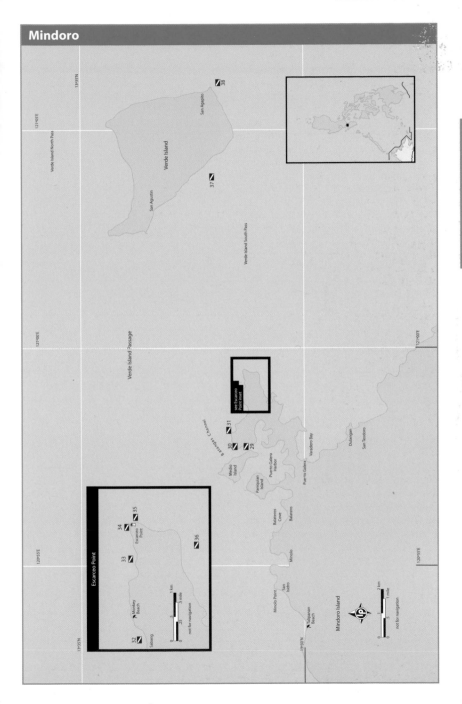

tropical topside as well as some of the best underwater scenery in the islands. The coastal waters of Puerto Galera were declared a marine sanctuary several decades ago. As a result, the reefs have become amazingly diverse and prolific over the years. The general consensus is that locals benefit more by maintaining and preserving the reefs and marine life, and by catering to divers' needs, than by fishing. Thus, you won't see dynamite damage on these reefs. A strong typhoon hit the area in 2006 and toppled a famous overhang at Pink Wall and stirred up some of the wooden wrecks. But overall, the many dive sites came out unscathed and some report an increase in diversity.

In the gorgeous coves and bays east of Puerto Galera you'll find more than 40 excellent dive sites within 20 minutes of most diving services, and more dive sites farther out. Accessible snorkeling is just offshore, where marine life abounds even in shallow water. There are also several worthwhile sites off Mindoro's west coast.

One of the interesting aspects of many Philippine beaches is that there are no piers so boats typically go as close to the beach as possible. Passengers scramble up or amble down a plank and then wade through knee-high and even chest-high water to get on and off. Sometimes the ladies are piggybacked by lean boatmen. So Puerto Galera gets some real kudos as at least one of the dive shops (Asia Divers) has a for-real pier that takes some of the circus act out of bangka boarding. There is also a sea wall that is used at high tide by a few of the other shops that simplifies entry and exit and keeps you dry.

Once on the boat, diving is possible year-round. Most Philippine diving is by outrigger although a few shops now have spacious speedboats. It's a toss up: the outriggers might be cheaper to operate and replace, but they are

slower and awkward to maneuver and to board and disembark. Some divers like the old charm; some like the speed and convenience of a fiberglass boat with big engines.

There are also a few possible shore entries. The waters are high in nutrients and current-fed corals thrive. Visibility can exceed 80ft, but is usually less. Currents can be quite strong at some of the sites, and unwary divers have been swept out to sea on occasion, so always dive with a knowledgeable local guide, of which there is no shortage.

This area is a huge technical-diving area. This book covers just the major sport-diving sites but there is also an array of deep (150ft+) sites that are regularly done with mixed gas and rebreathers.

Clam City has an array of giant tridacnas.

29	**CLAM CITY**

Location: *Puerto Galera Harbor*
Depth: *10-80ft (1-22m)*
Access: *Boat*
Range: *Novice*

Clam City is a fun site for macro and has its own local guard. Located in the channel southeast of Sabang, in Muele Bay, many giant tridacna clams have been placed for snorkelers to see and also to help reseed the area with giant clams. This was done by researchers from the University of Manila over a decade ago. As these can be tasty, a guard is posted in an anchored outrigger to ensure no one tries to get the meat for dinner.

So you know you are coming close to the site when you see a man sporting a broad umbrella in an outrigger bobbing off a buoy above a nice coral reef.

Sometimes the current can be strong here, but there are enough corals to hide behind that divers can easily explore. The shallows are interesting and you don't have to go any farther than 35ft to see plenty of macro life. Most of the clams are situated near reefs; a few are out in the sand. Since they feed by photosynthesis, they are in open, sunny water. Most are in 20ft or even less so snorkelers can be brought here to see them. Thus, there is a lot of boat traffic. So go up a mooring line and next to your guide's safety sausage.

In the clam area there are also many jawfish; sometimes two even share one hole. Look to see if any are incubating

The beautiful butterfly fish

eggs in their mouths. There are blue linkia starfish with small commensal shrimps, bubble anemones, snake eels, blue-spotted stingrays and bulldozer shrimp doing their thing as the sentinel goby watches warily. Look at about 30ft for one anemone that has a spinecheek clownfish with a flat head. Very odd.

Deeper in the channel, it's famous for macro critters. The coral cover disappears and a broad channel bottom stretches out. Look for roaming schools of catfish, seahorses, plume-worm colonies, solar-powered slugs, lizardfish and many other unusual creatures. Fish life swirls overhead as well.

This whole area is beautiful above the water as well as having some unique marine life down below. Sites such as Coral Gardens, the **Hills** (which is considered to be the shallower snorkeling area at Clam City) and even the populous **White Beach** all offer critter hunts.

White Beach is a local party hangout and there's lots of boat traffic. But its sandy bottom is known for good macro creatures such as ghost pipefish. Go with a good guide who knows how to safely exit and you may be surprised at the fish and invertebrate variety found on the sea floor at such a well-used beach.

30 CORAL GARDENS

Location: *Batangas Channel*
Depth: *10-50ft (3-15m)*
Access: *Boat*
Range: *Novice*

If you are heading by boat to any of the beaches northeast of Puerto Galera, you'll pass this attractive site on your way out of the channel near Long Beach.

Provided there's no current running, this is an easy dive that is frequently used for training and is also a great snorkeling spot. It has prolific hard corals and tube and encrusting sponges that grow in the shallow water. Staghorn and basket corals are also prolific, and shell fanciers will appreciate the variety of cowry species that are common at this site. Clams, morays, lionfish and the occasional frogfish also inhabit the area.

Photographers will also like this site as the shallow reef makes it easy to play with light for wide-angle scenes. Soft and hard corals make for colorful backdrops for fish and macro work.

31 | ALMA JANE

Location: *Directly off Asia Divers pier*
Depth: *40-100 ft (13-30m)*
Access: *Boat*
Range: *Advanced*

Sitting almost directly off the Asia Divers pier in Sabang Bay, this scuttled ship is a great fish magnet. It's the newest and most substantial wreck in the bay and could be dived from shore or the pier but is best done by boat as it is deep. The actual ship was a 60-ton, 115ft steel-hulled cargo ship. It was built in Japan in 1966 and was stripped of anything dangerous that would leak or hang up divers. When it was purposely sunk in March 2003, it landed upright, making it a great wreck to photograph as well as meaning that new wreck divers don't get disoriented easily.

A variety of marine life has taken up residence in and around the wreck, and wreckies and techies love having such an easily reachable ship to explore. Photographers love it even more, especially for wide-angle work.

There is usually a buoy aft, although these sometimes get stolen. Divers can descend all the way to the prop area in the back. The sand is at about 100ft, the deck 80ft and the upper bridge-type structure 55ft to 60ft. The prop has actually been removed but there is a rudder still intact and spotted sweetlips, snappers and batfish like to hover here. There is often current rolling over the ship, but you can hide from it if it's too stiff. Usually it's not bad and it's easy to swim down deep. Lots of photogenic baitfish and small wrasse can also be found deep aft.

Then move up to start exploring the holds. Most of the wire and stuff that could entangle a diver have been removed, but not all, so have fun poking around the insides but do be aware. One line that runs through the large

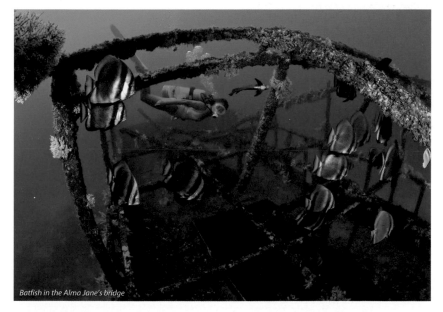

Batfish in the Alma Jane's bridge

Exploring the most intact of the Sabang wrecks

aft hold has some nice thick growth of colonial gorgonians. Cardinalfish also hide here. Lionfish are always in full attendance as there are large baitfish and fusilier schools that form thick shoals inside and give them plenty of food. Aside from the fish, the holds are open and empty and easy to swim around.

Snapper and batfish like the outside of the wreck and a school of yellowtail snapper is usually in the bow area. The batfish will be up in the bridge and wherever divers go – they seem to follow divers curiously. Looking up at the bow from the sand is a memorable experience and the water is normally clear out here so you can swim away a bit and look at the whole wreck.

There are remnants of a buoy line on the forward mast and you can just explore around the forward hold, mast

and the open bridge structure as you work your way up shallower. The batfish will play around the bridge area with you.

If you are shore diving you can start your swim back past the old wooden *St Christopher* wreck and up the sand slope and corals to the Asia Divers pier.

But this should really be a boat dive as the most fun when there is some current is to do an open-water drift ascent – at about 30ft to 40ft you should find a very large, flowing school of batfish. You can play with them and drift with them as you slowly make your way up to a decompression (deco) stop. This is a high traffic area. Make sure you or your guide have a large visible safety sausage and be sure to ascend close to the guide to avoid being whacked by a prop.

32   SABANG WRECKS

Location: *E of Sabang Point*
Depth: *10-70ft (3-22m)*
Access: *Boat or shore*
Range: *Novice inner beach, intermediate to advanced down to wrecks*

This dive is a lot of fun as it's fishy, has some reef and wreck action and can be either a wide-angle or a macro dive. It can be a walk-in from the sea grasses in the shallows by the floating bar, but it's easiest to grab a bangka ride out to a buoy that's attached to an anchor sitting down about 70ft.

Nearby is the stripped out hull of an old sailboat named *Awencha* and this is where you will probably be greeted by the ever-present batfish. The ship rests on it portside and is not really worth penetration unless you see some macro critters inside that you may want to photograph. Be careful of the scorpionfish and lionfish that inhabit the wreck if you are going to bump around inside – it's tight. There are also lots of cardinalfish inside.

Outside, lizardfish, encrusting sponges, soft corals and other invertebrates and clouds of anthias have made the old hull home.

From here swim south and up a meter or two and in between 52ft and 60ft you will find the tossed remains of a Vietnamese wooden vessel. It's pretty well leveled due to the years – and also the 2006 typhoon – but the ship's ribs are still present. Crinoids, rope sponges and anthias are all over this one as well. Also look for white-eye morays, frogfish and cuttlefish.

Moving on, with your batfish and surgeonfish entourage following, you'll find another wooden wreck that was once a Taiwanese fishing junk. Now the remnants are the home of a good number of cardinalfish and anthias. This small smorgasbord attracts the beautiful coral groupers (also seen on the *Awencha*) and lots of small damsels. There's still an old, encrusted engine, the ballast stones can be seen aft and part of the stern is still intact.

Look for cuttlefish and some butterflyfish and puffers around the wreck. Frogfish also conceal themselves well in the wooden ribs aft.

Now comes the critter and macro search. Start heading into the shallow part of the south bay where sand and sea grasses hold snake eels, stargazers, helmet gurnards, sea pens with small commensal crabs, ghost pipefish and arrays of chocolate-chip sea stars. This productive and interesting area is only

15ft to 20ft deep and you can do a long deco stop/critter search by scrounging around. This is a high-boat-traffic area so make sure you follow your guide up a safe mooring for your boat to pick you up. You don't want to pop up at the floating bar (or maybe you do!).

The sandy area down to the Taiwanese wreck makes for a very interesting night dive, when your chances of seeing a stargazer are pretty good. Many nocturnal fish and inverts can be seen at night making this – together with its closeness and ease – a very popular night dive.

33	WEST ESCARCEO

Location: *W of Escarceo Point*
Depth: *10-100ft (3-30m)*
Access: *Boat*
Range: *Novice/Intermediate*

Cryptic pygmy seahorse

Recovering Sunken Treasure

For centuries, Chinese traders and Spanish galleons roamed the often-perilous waters of the Philippines. Many ended up on the bottom of the ocean, their precious cargoes lost forever. Well, perhaps not forever…

Every year, discoveries of sunken treasures are announced – and more are kept tight-lipped secrets. While the odds are remote that you'll stumble onto an ancient Spanish galleon loaded with gold and jewels or a Chinese junk loaded to the gunwales with priceless Ming pottery, it can happen. And there's nothing like the thought of discovering a king's ransom in ancient treasure to add a little spice to a remote dive trip!

The remains of an ancient inter-island trading vessel are in many ways responsible for putting Puerto Galera on the diving map. This ship apparently caught fire and sunk hundreds of years ago. After identifying the wreck, discoverer Brian Homan and the National Museum salvaged Chinese pottery from the surrounding mud. Proceeds from the salvage project helped fund the area's fledgling dive centers, enabling them to expand and eventually capture a large share of the Philippines' diving market.

Not much is left of the wreck now, but Puerto Galera is a true diver's haven.

This site is a photographers' favorite for its normally calm waters at reeftop that hold beautiful hard brain, boulder and table corals and lots of small marine creatures. The dive then goes into a sharp slope that bottoms out at 100ft. Depending on the tide change and accompanying current, West Escarceo can be a relatively relaxing dive for a novice or a challenging one for an intermediate diver.

Bring a local guide to point out some of the critter haunts and also to be able to tell you if the current is changing in any way. The current can be fun as you may get pushed along the steep slope toward Hole in the Wall or you'll find yourself drifting among shoals of fusiliers and tuna. If it picks up it will take you all the way to Hole in the Wall or the Canyons. But if you want to just stay in the area, move back into the eddy area where things aren't moving so swiftly.

34	HOLE IN THE WALL

Location: *Off Escarceo Point*
Depth: *30-60ft (9-18m)*
Access: *Boat*
Range: *Novice*

When you enter this site, you will see the table corals below in consistently clear water. Drop down to 30ft and then slowly head down the reef after getting a good look at the stunning growth. The site is renowned for its sometimes ferocious currents and riptides, whirlpools and eddies. But that also accounts for the healthy coral cover that flows down the terraced and seemingly landscaped layered drop. That said, again, take an experienced guide.

This is a popular dive. The namesake Hole itself is not that deep, around 45ft, but is found under a ridge and can be missed if you don't follow the guide. You get there by swimming along several drop-offs festooned with hard and soft corals. The hole itself is about 5ft wide, which allows a fully equipped

Goby on soft coral

diver to easily pass through. Be careful not to brush the side as it's covered with brightly colored sponges, crinoids and soft corals.

The wall falls away beyond this to about 60ft and if the current isn't too strong you can explore the whole area. Keep an eye out into the blue for large pelagics – local divers have from time to time reported seeing mantas, whale sharks and other big fish here and at the adjacent Canyons.

You have a good chance of seeing hawksbill and green sea turtles beyond the hole. You will certainly see sweetlips and lionfish, probably jacks and dogtooth tuna, moray eels and maybe even a sleeping whitetip shark. Head back up around a point at about 50ft and through a series of coral heads and sand. Finish up at the same pretty tabletop coral area where you entered and move up shallow for a deco stop.

35 THE CANYONS

Location: *Off Escarceo Point*
Depth: *25-130ft (8-40m)*
Access: *Boat*
Range: *Advanced*

An advanced site, Canyons has always been one of the popular adrenalin dives. Local knowledge of the currents is imperative here, as you must rely on the prevailing current to sweep you into position on this dive. After racing with the current over several small drop-offs festooned with big golden gorgonians and past thick schools of golden anthias, soft corals and sponges, you'll find yourself in an area with several crevasses (the Canyons) that are cleft into the wall. These afford some respite from the usually raging current.

You may find it funny to look around and see a lot of hunkering sweetlips, emperor angelfish and grunts hiding from the current right beside you.

Expect to see large schools of trevallies, snappers, barracuda and sometimes whitetip sharks. Lionfish, surgeonfish and lined angelfish are also often present. There's lots going on as the currents always seem to make the ocean creatures come alive with activity.

The usual end point of this dive is a large anchor, about 5ft across, embedded in the reef. It's covered with soft corals and is home to a couple of lionfish. You may get lucky here and spot the legendary Barnacle Bill, a large hawksbill turtle that frequents the area.

Remembering John Bennett

One of the sport's most famous deep divers lived and practiced his world-record swims along the reefs at Puerto Galera. John Bennett set records for diving on air and on mixed gas and is credited with pushing the sport to new limits with his inventive mixed-gas theories. His first world-record dive was set off the shores of Puerto Galera while he was an instructor at Captain Gregg's.

In the next few years he dove to an incredible 1000ft, experiencing a look at the depths few will ever know. John was always an enthusiastic student of scuba and willing to talk about his take on the extreme end of the sport with anyone seriously interested. He was a teacher, father and good guy.

Sadly, John died in what was a pretty routine salvage job in Korea in 2002. His body was never found so the exact cause was never known. But his legacy lives on in Puerto Galera with the limits he dared to break off the Mindoro shores.

The Canyons have golden sea fans

36   SINADIGAN WALL

Location: *SW of Escarceo Point*
Depth: *10-130ft (3-40m)*
Access: *Boat*
Range: *Intermediate*

Tube corals in an overhang

This is an interesting dive with two walls, a wide variety of marine life from tiny nudibranchs to the occasional pelagic and some shallow end-of-dive swim-throughs that make for great photos.

Start by entering at about 15ft and then slowly make your way down the reef slope. There is an interesting coral valley that leads to the first wall in about 45ft of water. This dive has some nice wide-angle possibilities but is famous for its nudibranch diversity. You'll see lots of Chromodoris, Nembrotha, Glossodoris, Hyselodoris, Flabellina and flatworms among many more. So look close as you cruise past the many coral heads and along the big and small walls.

The usual suspects of tropical reef fish call this home, and occasionally pelagics pass by, especially when the current is running. Look for surgeonfish, lionfish, groupers, snappers, a few morays and the odd pufferfish. This is also a good site for sea snakes.

Most divers favor a longer shallow swim here looking for sea life, but down deep in the valley between the two walls is a rock at 131ft called **Turtle Rock**. It's down here you might see some of the bigger pelagics out in the blue.

The second wall is about 45ft deep up to 20ft or so and is toward the end of the dive. There are snapper schools and yellow damsels and lots of anemones – including one rather toxic anemone that looks like a piece of turf. Don't touch it but it usually has a couple of very photogenic commensal shrimp in it. Small yellow sea cucumbers are thick as are crinoids in all colors and sizes. Sweetlips and shoals of juvenile catfish roam the reef. There are also some very scenic overhangs with beautiful *Tubastreas* covering the upper part of the tunnel. These open up when there is current and are amazingly colorful, in yellows and rich salmon.

The cliffs fall right into the sea here and boulders and swim-throughs can be found all along the upper reef in 4ft to 15ft of water. This is a great studio with sun rays beaming through the clear water. You can even see the clouds. All in all this is a fascinating and diverse site.

Crinoids thrive at Washing Machine

37 | WASHING MACHINE

Location: *Off Verde Island's west tip*
Depth: *10-50ft (3-15m)*
Access: *Boat*
Range: *Advanced*

Verde Island is a small island across from Puerto Galera between the provinces of Batangas and Mindoro. Verde Island Passage is a very busy shipping lane with a lot of ferry and barge traffic. There is not much development on Verde Island as it is a private, family-owned bamboo plantation. Bamboo covers most of the island.

This dive is located at the island's northwest tip and is great for big barrel sponges. It's a wild drift when the current is running. As the name implies, the current can be pretty wild and mixed-up, putting the diver through a wash-and-rinse cycle during the course of the dive. While this site may not be everybody's cup of tea, when the current is running at full tilt, the Washing Machine is like a crazy amusement park ride.

The fun occurs over a series of seven gullies on the gently sloping seafloor that runs out from the rocky shore of Verde's west coast. When the current is running, you fairly fly over the bottom, swooping down into a gully to get out of the raging torrent whenever you feel like taking a break.

However, when the current's not running, it's like a walk in the park – so if enjoying the marine life is more your thing, don't let the name fool you. It can be very nice before the tide starts to move. For those who would like to explore a nicely decorated reef with big barrel sponges, spiny pufferfish, lots of colorful crinoids and a bunch of sea anemones, just go at slack tide.

This makes for a leisurely swim to many points of interest along a sloping hill of scattered corals that leads to a sand valley in relatively shallow water. But always take a guide just in case you decide to be leisurely and the tide does pick up. They will let you know when the ride is about to begin.

There is nothing particularly impressive about what comes into this site other than the current – there are really no fish schools or pelagics to see most of the time.

38 | VERDE ISLAND WALL

Location: *SE point of Verde Island*
Depth: *15-100ft (4-30m)*
Access: *Boat*
Range: *Intermediate*

If you have the opportunity to dive twice here, do so. This is one of the best wall dives in the country. Although closer to Puerto Galera and popular with divers based there, Verde is also regularly visited by divers staying in Anilao and can be dived from the island's own resort and dive center.

The wall itself is easy to find: look for the two rocks jutting out of the sea off the island's southeast point. Drop in a few meters south of them, then head north, but be careful of the current, which can whisk you away in the wrong direction if you plan your dive poorly. The visibility is usually excellent here and the wall itself has lots of cracks and crevices that you can use to duck out of the current, but remember that it falls away to great depths. Most divers remain above 80ft and, frankly, there is no good reason to descend any deeper than that. It's not a sheer wall and coral growth is dense and diverse.

The wall itself is festooned in an impossible array of colorful corals. Some especially impressive gorgonians decorate the wall, jutting out between vast slabs of star corals. Huge, colorful riots of soft corals drape and dangle from the drop-off, and sea fans and anemones sway endlessly in the current.

Whitetips and other sharks, occasional mantas, eagle rays, tuna and jacks, rainbow runners, wahoo and Spanish mackerel are among the pelagics you might hope to see along this exciting wall.

You are most likely to see Napoleon wrasse, parrotfish, unicornfish, legions of soldierfish, surgeons, batfish, tangs, sweetlips and emperors throughout the area. Many fish hide behind bommies down deeper to avoid or enjoy the current and can be quite well-fed and large. Look for gobies in the sand. There are also clouds of anthias everywhere making the whole place move with color.

When making your recommended safety stop on top of the reef, there are some very nice shallow coral gardens with chromis hovering. Also, the reef belches occasionally! Look for the bubbles of volcanic gases escaping from cracks in the reef.

Anthias and healthy gorgonian fans

Sibuyan Sea Dive Sites

This region is a live-aboard destination that has a couple of unique spots. Three-day trips or weekenders are the norm.

The Sibuyan Sea lies between the east coast of Mindoro, the west coast of Bicol, the south coast of Marinduque Island and the northern Visayas. Though it's too remote to be dived by day boats, live-aboard trips to the area are organized by dive centers from Puerto Galera, Boracay and now Donsol and usually last from three to five days.

Yet, due to unpredictable weather patterns and sea conditions, schedules sometimes change. The diving season runs from January to June, with March to May being the best months to visit, but it's possible to dive year-round at some of the more sheltered sites.

Dive sites here are varied, ranging from the popular wreck of the MV *Mactan* (an inter-island ferryboat that went down off the coast of Maestre de Campo a few decades ago) to tiny colorful Banton Island and the sheltered Romblon and Tablas Islands. The waters surrounding Marinduque are home to a number of more sheltered sites, such as Tres Reyes, Dos Hermanos and Nantanco, which are usually only visited when the seas are too rough to get to preferred destinations.

Sibuyan Sea Dive Sites	GOOD SNORKELING	NOVICE	INTERMEDIATE	ADVANCED
39 MV *MACTAN* FERRY & JAPANESE WRECKS	•	•		
40 BANTON BIG ROCK CORAL GARDEN	•		•	
41 BANTON NW AND BANTON SW WALLS	•		•	

39 MV MACTAN FERRY & JAPANESE WRECKS

Location: *NE of Maestre de Campo Island*
Depth: *82-130ft (25-40m)*
Access: *Live-aboard boat*
Range: *Intermediate*

Sibuyan Sea

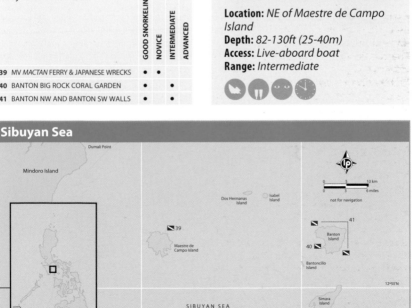

This old ferryboat capsized in the late '70s in a freak wave just off the coast of Maestre de Campo Island. The passengers and crew, many of whom, no doubt, were not swimmers, were saved by hauling themselves along a rope that a couple of brave swimmers managed to attach to the sinking vessel from the mainland. No lives were lost, and the diving community gained one of the country's better wreck dives.

The hull sits more or less upright and north to south on the 82ft to 180ft deep sandy bottom. It's now home to groupers, snappers, sweetlips, shoals of barracuda, plenty of lionfish and lots of small tropical reef fish. The wreck is penetrable, but because of its depth, only experienced and trained wreck divers should attempt to do so. It's an excellent technical dive. Current can be a factor here, and though the visibility is not always perfect, it can reach more than 65ft.

Maestre de Campo's harbor, Port Concepcion, is the final resting place of the remains of two small Japanese warships and a couple of small WWII planes. Visibility is not normally that good here, but the muddy seabed can often reward a diligent searcher with a relic or bottle to photograph and return to the sea bed. The west side of the island boasts some decent coral gardens, good for a second dive or snorkeling when the sea is calm.

40	**BANTON BIG ROCK CORAL GARDEN**

Location: *Banton Island's west coast*
Depth: *0-40ft (0-13m)*
Access: *Live-aboard boat*
Range: *Novice*

Clown triggerfish

After diving Banton's Northwest Wall, head southwest around the corner to a small bay with a large rock sticking out of it. This is a colorful shallow dive – you needn't exceed 40ft – and is also an excellent snorkeling site.

Swim over the pristine coral reef, where sea whips and a host of other corals – table, boulder, brain and more – carpet the sandy seafloor. Groupers, snappers, sweetlips, cuttlefish and lots of small reef fish are everywhere, and they don't seem overly shy of divers or snorkelers. The large rock's seaward face has a huge cleft that is penetrable for several meters.

41	**BANTON NW & BANTON SW WALLS**

Location: *Banton NW and SW*
Depth: *0-130ft (0-40m)*
Access: *Live-aboard boat*
Range: *Intermediate*

Long, deep and alive. About 30km from Marinduque Island's southern tip, Banton is a nearly circular island with a diameter of just 3km. The islanders rely on copra farming for subsistence (the entire island is covered in coconut trees), and they don't maintain a fishing fleet: in fact, they discourage off-islanders from fishing in their waters. Although serious currents can rip around the island, and it's not always possible to reach it in a small boat, once you get there, you can usually dive on one side of the island or the other.

Though the island has two main sites and a number of lesser ones, **Banton's Northwest Wall** is one of the most impressive in the country. And it's easy to find – just get in the water a few meters offshore from the graffiti written on the cliff by a rather overzealous scholastic-fraternity member.

Huge gorgonians, sheer slopes, overhangs, cracks, caves, crevices, some outstanding hard- and soft-coral formations and a host of reef and pelagic fish make this relatively short section of the rugged Banton Island coast a place that divers want to visit again and again. You'll always find something new, whether it be a manta ray, sharks, Napoleon wrasses, tuna, barracuda, sweetlips, large groupers or snappers. Look for soldierfish and surgeons swimming in shoals, pennant butterflyfish flitting about, morays poking out of holes and pufferfish puffing around. Gobies, blennies, anthias and chromis weave their way in and out of the soft corals, table gorgonians and other stony corals that adorn the wall.

The **Banton Southeast Wall** is an alternative when the current or waves are too much to dive the Northwest Wall. A gently sloping healthy coral garden runs from the seashore to around 33ft, where the wall drops off steeply. Some good overhangs, crevices and some really big soft corals cascade in places over the lip of the wall, forming bulbous pastel curtains. You'll find plenty of fish, but the visibility is not usually as good here as at Northwest Wall.

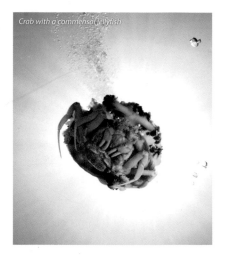
Crab with a commensal jellyfish

The Visayas Dive Sites

Some of the most famous beaches in the Philippines are found here in this scattering of islands both big and small. Once a secret, closely guarded by European tourists, this area has blossomed into a holiday favorite. Divers fly into Cebu City and branch out to their favorite dive areas looking for thresher sharks, rare macro critters, shipwrecks or all of the above. Some of the best snorkeling sites in the Philippines are also found here.

The ships in the seas around the Visayas are like a history display of maritime vessels: everything from super-modern fast cats to aging wooden hulks go from port to port. Many of the resort islands now have commuter flights for those with a bit less romance and more practicality in their itinerary.

BORACAY

Just a couple of decades ago Boracay was left to sun-ripe Europeans and the hippie fringe. Nowadays, it's the poster region for snow-white beaches, emerald waters and upscale resorts. It attracts Filipinos escaping the big city of Manila and tourists escaping all the other big cities of the world.

Along the west-facing beach are more than 30 dive centers, a variety of resorts both large and small and hip boutiques. The range of food is incredible, with a taste for every palate. You can golf, sail, ride banana boats and dance well into the night at thumping late-night clubs.

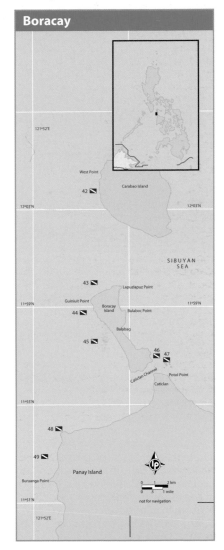

Boracay

The Visayas Boracay	GOOD SNORKELING	NOVICE	INTERMEDIATE	ADVANCED
42 CATHEDRAL CAVE			•	
43 YAPAK				•
44 PUNTA BONGA 1 & 2		•	•	
45 FRIDAY'S ROCK		•	•	
46 CROCODILE ISLAND		•	•	
47 LAUREL ISLAND 1 & 2		•	•	
48 NASOG POINT		•	•	
49 DOG DRIFT		•	•	

Fire goby

But when not shopping, dining and disco dancing, there's diving. Boracay's geography provides for a number of sheltered dive sites. January through June is the optimum dive time but the range of sites means divers can visit year-round.

The numerous dive shops offer a wide array of training. Even instructor development courses (IDC) and tech diving are taught here. Dives such as Yapak that start at 100ft are great for tech dives using mixed gas.

'You can get there from here' is the motto. Numerous small aircraft jockey between the islands to airstrips at Caticlan on Panay Island and Kalibo airport.

For those wanting to see more, liveaboards in the area also visit the further-flung dive sites in the Sibuyan Sea in season (which can be tricky).

42	CATHEDRAL CAVE

Location: *West Carabao Island*
Depth: *82-130ft (25-40m)*
Access: *Boat*
Range: *Intermediate*

To get to this site you must cross the unpredictable channel to Carabao Island. Seas get big quickly so this isn't always for the faint of heart. But those who love a unique dive swear by Cathedral Cave.

This is a huge, yawning cavern that starts at 80ft and extends far into the reef wall. It's not so deep and dark that cave-diving training is needed, but bring a good light. The blue hue of the entrance is always in sight.

Poke around the walls and cracks to see what's in there on any given day. Fish swim upside own, orienting themselves to the cave walls. *Tubastrea* and black corals grow from the ceiling.

Look for the occasional huge grouper that may have wandered in for a nap or a meal. Whitetips like to rest on the bottom and small schools of hunting trevally are on patrol.

This is the largest, but not the only, cave or crevice along this wall. Look for nice coral growth along the walls and shoaling fish in the water column.

43 | YAPAK

Location: *N of Boracay*
Depth: *100-130ft (30-40m)*
Access: *Boat*
Range: *Intermediate*

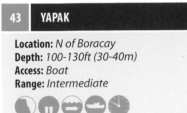

This is a good spot for Mr Big Deep and for the more-experienced diver, because of the currents, which attract large fish, this can be a very colorful dive. The wall is full of gorgonian sea fans and soft corals. The barrel sponges and clouds of smaller fish can divert a diver's attention.

But it's best to look into the blue if you want to see whitetip and blacktip sharks. Hammerheads and even an occasional whale shark have also been spotted.

But wait, there's more. Yellowfin and dogtooth tuna, jacks, roaming wahoo, blackbar barracuda, Spanish mackerel and all of those current-loving bluewater fish are part of the parade.

There must be a lot of food in these waters, as even mantas pass by. Again, this is for experienced divers only, who have had deep-diving training and plenty of deep-dive experience. The depth combined with the currents can lead to problems very quickly. Punta

Bonga offers good pelagic action at shallower depths so consider that if Yapak is a bit over your head.

44 | PUNTA BONGA 1 & 2

Location: *N of Friday's Rock, West Boracay*
Depth: *26-130ft (8-40m)*
Access: *Boat*
Range: *Intermediate*

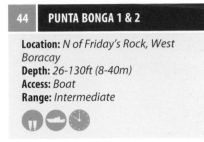

Punta Bonga 1 is the shallower of these two dives. The dive spot starts fairly shallow and drops off to the depths. The wall is closer to shore and more pronounced than the slopes south of this site. Look for a nice, healthy selection of hard corals, swaying soft corals and lots of smaller fish.

Punta Bonga 2 has similar cover but is ledgy and cascades down in broad steps to deeper water. Look for tuna, bigeye jacks, schools of blackbar-barracuda and wandering whitetips along this site. The corals are home to beautifully marked clown triggerfish, striped sweetlips, trumpetfish and cornetfish.

This isle also a good place to find large marble rays, which sometimes get completely covered in sand as they sleep or lay in wait on the sea floor.

Red fang triggerfish

Fish and large table coral

45 FRIDAY'S ROCK

Location: *Just off Balabag,
West Boracay*
Depth: *23-60ft (7-18m)*
Access: *Shore (long swim) or boat*
Range: *All Levels*

46 CROCODILE ISLAND

Location: *Off Boracay's southeastern
tip*
Depth: *16-82ft (5-25m)*
Access: *Boat*
Range: *Intermediate*

The Boracay dive shops use this site for all kinds of dive training. It can be reached by entering from the shore or by bangka. However, the swim from shore is a bit far – not bad on the way out but tiring on the way back, so boat is the recommended approach.

The actual Friday's Rock is submerged. This big coral boulder is about 38ft high with lots of fish living in and around it. A coral garden also rises up into the shallows nearby.

Fish feeding has been introduced here, so fish photographers should have a good time snapping the many multi-hued tropicals that come around for a free meal. Look for striped snappers, various species of butterflyfish, groupers, damsels and curious wrasses.

The sandy bottom is home to ribbon eels in all stages from blue to black to the aging yellow; it is scattered with smaller rocks and camouflaged scorpionfish; and is a favorite habitat of flowing lionfish.

From the right angle, Crocodile Island looks like a big knobby croc. Snorkelers love the site for its nice corals and variety of fish life in the shallows. Those good at breath-hold can even slip over the wall and find gorgonians and other pretty corals in fairly shallow waters.

Current fed, it attracts a nice diversity of fish. This may be because the site sits at the eastern mouth of the Caticlan Channel, which divides Boracay from the mainland. Divers will like the wall for the gorgonians, sea whips and good coral diversity highlighted by a 'gazillion' anthias.

The rocky island is known for its sea snakes so don't be surprised if you see a banded sea snake on a dive. Reef fish you might see here include roaming shoals of fusiliers, Moorish idols, various sweetlips, butterflyfish, triggerfish and members of the parrotfish family.

Look closely at the reef and you'll see a nice selection of nudibranchs, including some of the Chromodoris family.

Banded pipefish

Anthias in hard coral

47 | LAUREL ISLAND 1 & 2

Location: *SE of Crocodile Island*
Depth: *10-65ft (3-20m)*
Access: *Boat*
Range: *Intermediate*

The big attraction here is the fish life and coral growth. This is a good spot for snorkeling as many coral come close to the surface and there are nice coral gardens at both sites. There can be a current running from slight to quite strong, so check the conditions so you aren't taken by surprise. Both sites 1 and 2 are in the Caticlan Channel and the flow keeps the corals well fed and healthy.

The actual dives aren't that deep and each has fish life and visibility similar to Crocodile Island with not a lot of pelagics. There is some big, old-growth coral that gives the impression this has been a healthy and thriving reef for quite some time.

But **Laurel Island 1** has a special feature – a tunnel about 25ft (8m) long that blossoms when the current is running as it is full of bright salmon, yellow and orange *Tubastrea* corals. This is an eye-popping display. It gets even better as you emerge into a large bowl that drops down to the reef bottom at around a civil 60ft. The bowl is adorned in hard corals, soft black coral trees and large bommies.

Laurel Island 2 also has similar corals and great fish life. Both are very photogenic and photographers like to try both wide angle and macro. Either one can also be recommended for a night dive.

Nasog Point is a regional favorite and Boracay dive centers like to combine this with a dive at nearby Dog Drift.

49 | DOG DRIFT

Location: *S of Nasog Point*
Depth: *16-100ft (5-30m)*
Access: *Boat*
Range: *Intermediate*

Don't ask how this site got its name. It's an easy assumption that the dog wasn't too happy about the situation. It's an easy drift dive with or without canine companionship.

This small, but packed, wall has many caves, crevices and holes to explore that serve as habitat for a lot of marine life including spiny lobsters, resting sea turtles and reclusive blennies.

Keep an eye out in the blue, as pelagic fish are known to drift into the water column to have a look at divers.

The reef is similar to nearby Nasog Point, but the fish life here is more prolific. Groupers, snapper schools and some batfish are among the residents, while the cracks and crevices also hold moray eels. Lionfish can be seen here too – sometimes they are upside down resting on the underside of an overhang. Stonefish blend in perfectly with the reef here, so watch what you grab.

It's a slow and easy drift in moderate current, where you can stop and go and see a lot of marine life.

48 | NASOG POINT

Location: *NW Panay*
Depth: *0-115ft (0-35m)*
Access: *Boat*
Range: *Intermediate*

This site is a little different than some of the others, as its bottom is littered with a maze of big boulders, deep canyons and lots of coral cover and gorgonian sea fans. Soft corals also open up when the current is moderate and paint the site with color.

Fish life isn't as good as at Crocodile, but there is a better chance of seeing pelagic fish swim by. Dogtooth tuna, barracuda and even an eagle ray may make an appearance.

Hawksbill sea turtle

MALAPASCUA ISLAND

This Visayas area continues to get more interesting as divers better explore the fantastic sites available. The hub for travel to the island is Cebu City. The Mactan-Cebu International Airport handles both domestic and international flights. Public transport is available to Malapascua, but it's a bone-jarring ride that is done much better by private car or minivan. Expect to pay around US$65 for the three-hour trip to the town of Maya in a nice, air-con car that is called a taxi but is much better. Have your dive shop line this up and you can be met at the airport or jet-ferry dock. Try to time your arrival in Maya so you can start the half-hour crossing to the island before dark. So, you need to leave Cebu City no later than 2pm or so.

The trip is a pleasant one that goes north out of the city, past its extended 'burbs and then along the ocean. Here you will see some seaside resorts, which are especially popular on weekends with Cebu City vacationers. The road then heads away from the coast and into the farmlands. It winds over the hills and rolling valleys past fields of sugarcane. Baked goods and local candy are hawked alongside the road as the scenery and people turn delightfully rural. You may pass cowboys on horseback and fields of grazing cattle. For the most part, the road is good hardtop but being worked on in spots.

Make sure you have alerted your dive shop on Malapascua of your approximate arrival time to have a vessel waiting or you will have to haggle for a ride to the island. When you get to the tiny port of Maya, you will probably be confronted by 'porters' who

Malapascua Island

Malapascua Island Dive Sites	GOOD SNORKELING	NOVICE	INTERMEDIATE	ADVANCED
50 GATO ISLAND		•	•	
51 NORTH POINT		•		•
52 BANTIGUE		•		•
53 THE SAND PATCH		•		•
54 MONAD SHOAL		•		•
55 CALANGGAMAN		•		•
56 *DONA MARILYN* WRECK		•		•
57 *LIGHTHOUSE* WRECK & LIGHTHOUSE WEST		•	•	
58 *TAPILON* WRECK				•

may insist on carrying your bags the short distance to your ship. Be sure to count your bags when they have been deposited on your outrigger as these guys aren't really certified porters and just hang around for a quick buck. Pay about P20 for each bag carried. Beware of scams in Maya and don't pay more that P1500 for a boat crossing unless it is bad weather. It's best to make arrangements in advance with your dive shop – then you won't have any hassles.

Be careful boarding your boat. For some reason, the ships from Malapascua have the narrowest ramps of anywhere in the Philippines. The crew is usually there to help with this maneuver, but it's a bit of a tightrope act.

As Maya gets smaller in the distance, islands become closer and the rocky coast of south Malapascua, combined with long stretches of white-sand beaches and the towering palms of Bounty Beach, beckon you to tropical paradise. There are no cars out here and few cycles. It's quiet and friendly. You see people walking along sandy patches and hotels are all beachfront. It's a magical little island, with many beaches and coves that are certainly among the best in the Philippines. A broad inner lagoon and sea-grass area provides a breeding ground to a great variety of marine life and the island has some nice shallow hard-coral areas for snorkelers as well.

Walk around the island when you get spare time and visit with the people in the village. About 3000 islanders live here, although you don't really notice that many people. They are very friendly and open to conversation. They speak a local dialect, but also English.

The restaurants are excellent – don't miss Angelina's for the finest in Italian food. Oscar's at Thresher Shark Divers offers a new dinner menu daily, fresh fruit juices and two-for-one happy-

hour drinks. And once you get there you will see the thresher-shark theme everywhere. Carvings, T-shirts, paintings on boats… the thresher is king here. The carvings are very nice and done by one or two local carvers – they also do mantas.

The drop-offs and seamounts of this island, along with nearby Gato Island, provide some great pelagic experiences. Monad Shoal is the famous seamount, and many prolific macro sites have also been identified. Add to this the presence of diveable war wrecks and a sunken ferry and it's easy to see why this sleepy hideaway is becoming one of the Philippines' most popular.

Puffer hiding in leather coral

Gato has a tunnel that goes completely through the island
Photo Yoko Higashide

50 | GATO ISLAND

Location: *40mins NW of Malapascua*
Depth: *16-82ft (5-25m)*
Access: *Boat*
Range: *Intermediate*

Gato Island sits off in the distance a little northwest of Malapascua and is a popular all-day destination. Normally two dives will be done at this site in one day, or else a single dive following a dive at the *Dona Marilyn* wreck north of Gato. Otherwise, a three-dive day can be done entirely here, or as two dives here with a third at Malapascua on the way back. Whatever the plan, the dives here are good and full of diversity.

The island is a marine reserve and designated as a sea-snake sanctuary. There's a ranger station perched precariously high up on the island's rocks. The rangers and researchers welcome any fresh fruit or vegetable offerings.

There are about five dive sites with varying terrain and marine life – the macro life is particularly good. Divers can drift along the high rock walls, explore the undercuts and small caves, swim between the rocks and hide in the lee for leisurely exploration. There are many options – wide-angle photography may be good for one dive (you might want to take your wide-angle on the swim-through, as the cave mouth makes a nice frame) while there is enough macro fun for at least a couple of dives. The sandy bottom flattens out around 80ft but dives can be done anywhere between 15ft and 60ft with great success. It's not necessary to go really deep to see a lot.

Look for banded sea snakes, of course, as well as cuttlefish. They mate and hover on the bottom and even catch fish here if you stop to watch their act.

The undercuts hold large black coral trees. In these you will find arrow crabs, anthias, lionfish and lots of other creatures taking refuge in the wispy coral. Look for many different type of black coral *(Antipathes sp)* around the island, including the beautiful white-bottle-brush black coral.

The island also has a unique feature: a novelty dive. This is a swim-through that goes completely across the island. The **Cave** dive normally starts by entering on the island's west side. It's really a long tunnel. The shallow part of the dive starts by swimming between some big boulders at about 15ft to 20ft. More than a pair of divers can fit side by side in the big entrance. There is also a rope at the tunnel roof. Look at the unusual sponge growths along the walls, and the black corals.

The Cave does get a bit deeper as one goes through it and the blue glimmer of the entrance disappears just before the blue glimmer of the exit appears. You need a guide and a light and it's about a five- to 10-minute swim through to the other side of the island.

This 100ft-long tunnel houses all the usual cave dwellers, such as decorator crabs, painted lobsters and usually some large pufferfish. The Cave is also home to whitetip sharks, which seem to add to the thrill factor. The whitetips like to rest inside or near the opening and let the current run over their gills. The sharks will begrudgingly move aside, but divers may find them pretty much in their way as they try to pass by to get out. There aren't as many whitetips around as there used to be but there are still some, as well as cat and bamboo sharks.

The exit is at about 50ft. There is a gorgonian fan or two outside that holds pygmy seahorses. Divemasters try to time the dive so you can drift back to the boat easily with the current.

For macro freaks, try the **Guardhouse**. This area has many boulders full of tiny things such as urchins with urchin shrimp, many nudibranchs, *Tubastrea* corals and anemones. Many anemones are crowded with clownfish. Also, painted frogfish seem to come and go here, so look closely at what might not be a sponge.

Pygmy Seahorses

The seahorses that are found around the Philippines aren't always that easy to see, because many are members of the pygmy-seahorse family and blend in perfectly with golden gorgonian or purplish-looking *Muricella sp* sea fans. The seahorses don't move much, and they take on the color of the fan and so are easily overlooked by the casual diver.

Bring a small light and look for yellow or red dots of a slightly different color than the sea fan. Sometimes the curly tail the sea horse uses to hold onto that fan is the giveaway. Then take a closer look – there may be more than one. Sometimes there can be a dozen pygmies in just one small part of a fan.

Use a 105mm lens to see them and have your guide help so you can snap some shots, then leave them be. They stress easily if they get too much exposure to bright lights, such as flashlights or strobes.

Soft coral hanging from an undercut

51 | NORTH POINT

Location: *North tip of Malapascua, 5mins by boat*
Depth: *18-70ft (5-22m)*
Access: *Boat*
Range: *Intermediate*

This is an interesting dive site with varied terrain and a variety of sea creatures to see. A series of ridges, which are undercut and covered with brilliant soft corals, lead to sandy plains. There is also a large boulder near the mooring that is adorned in brilliant orange soft coral and a coral garden of leather corals that stretches for a long drift.

As it's at the point, it's completely different when the current is running for a tide change than it is at slack tide. In the current, the beautiful soft coral really opens up and the reef is more colorful. But the current is strong and it's a bit of work getting to the habitats of some of the small marine life, which includes giant and clown frogfish in many colors, fire urchins with their commensal crabs or shrimp, nudibranchs and even a couple of *Muricella sp* sea fans with pygmy seahorses.

Whether the current is running or not, end the dive at the large coral garden. Puffers rest in the huge leather corals and the healthy reef stretches for a nice swim or drift up into the shallows for a decompression (deco) stop. You may find yourself drifting at deco here. Follow the guide and his safety sausage and look for some big jellyfish that sometimes blow into the area and have small jacks hiding in their tentacles.

52 | BANTIGUE

Location: *North tip of Malapascua, 5mins by boat*
Depth: *18-65ft (5-18m)*
Access: *Boat*
Range: *Intermediate*

53 | THE SAND PATCH

Location: *North tip of Malapascua, 5mins by boat*
Depth: *18-65ft (5-18m)*
Access: *Boat*
Range: *Novice*

This is considered a muck dive locally but is also a good wide-angle and fish dive. It's a fascinating area with a bit of everything stretched across a rolling plain with a miniwall: tons of anemones, a sandy slope full of elegant filamented male sand divers and lots more. You can get good results with a wide angle such as 12mm to 24mm, or a 60mm or 105mm macro.

Follow the guide as you check out sponges and sea fans and a small cave that holds a giant frogfish, lionfish and a mass of baitfish. Then swim across a sandy plain to a ridge dotted with cotton-candy and curly-wire corals, and sea fans. The gorgonians also hold pygmy seahorses.

You will end the dive admiring the many sea anemones, cotton-candy gorgonians, various nudibranchs and other marine life going up into the shallows.

This shallow dive is like a treasure hunt across sandy plains and into sea grasses that hold all kind of odd and cool macro critters. The area is normally protected, with not much in the way of currents, and it's shallow, so long dives can be made – and you never know what will pop up next.

The sand holds an assortment of nudi-branchs, guaranteed smashing-mantis shrimp in tiny and not-so-tiny holes, comical-looking devil scorpionfish, wire-coral shrimp, pipefish, decorator crabs, anemone hermit crabs, Pegasus sea moths, chocolate-chip sea stars, juvenile catfish schools and lots more.

There are a number of sand anemones with lots of clownfish and shrimp that may try to clean you.

This is also a good place to see a variety of gobies and their bulldozer shrimp. Mimic octopuses have also been spotted here. Good luck!

Commensal shrimp on a linkia starfish

A pair of yellow gobies in sea grasses

54 MONAD SHOAL

Location: *E of Malapascua*
Depth: *50-130ft (15-40m)*
Access: *Boat*
Range: *Intermediate*

Monad Shoal isn't just any old seamount. An underwater island due east of Malapascua, it's about a half-hour boat ride in calm seas – and dive guides on the island are used to rising early as this is the site divers flock to for early-morning sightings of thresher sharks on the edge of a 600ft (200m) drop-off.

It's famous as the only place in the world where thresher sharks can be seen on a reasonably consistent basis, though not daily. They are seen at cleaning stations perched along the outer edge of the drop-off and they like to clean around sunrise. So the daily parade of bleary-eyed divers stumbling onto dive boats before dawn is a given at Malapascua. It's actually a very pleasant time of day, with the soft light and sun rising over the dive site. Buoys have been put in place leading down close to the cleaning stations.

The process is simple. Go down the mooring line, swim over close to the cleaning station, stay low so as not to scare or interfere with the sharks, kneel down on the reeftop and peer into the blue waiting for something big or unusual to show up. This is a perfect dive for Nitrox as it extends bottom time, reduces the chance of getting into deco and gives you more time at the station to see if a shark wanders in. There are a couple of main cleaning sites along the steep wall.

It's a very challenging environment for underwater photographers as visibility seems to change at these venues every two minutes. It's already dark down there – even at noon – as it's

A huge jellyfish at Monad Shoal is shelter for juvenile jacks

nutrient-rich water, and the way the station sits, you're kind of shooting into the sun. Visibility may be 20m when you descend, then go down to as little at 5m before getting clearer again – very unpredictable. Set your ISO for as high as possible, to get as much light as you can. As if all that's not problematic enough, the sharks are hard to approach, so they rarely get in very close.

To top it all off, strobes aren't allowed. The strobe ban was a decision reached by all the dive-shop operators together in 2008 because shark sightings were declining and they wanted to put some diving etiquette in place. It seems to have worked, as shark numbers have been steadily increasing since the ban was instituted. This makes sense, as some photographers carry powerful strobes and attempt to shoot at full power instead of using a low-powered fill, and such bright flashes often startle sea creatures, including molas and other deep-water sharks.

Sharks often swim away when they are flashed, and if one photographer scares a shark off for the rest of the group, that means a bunch of unhappy divers (and, if you are that photographer, you feel like hiding your camera). So this ban is a bit of an assurance of peace among divers as well. Furthermore, the shop owners point out that little real research has been done on the threshers, so they don't know how it might affect the population long-term if they are constantly flashed every morning – the shops certainly don't want them to change cleaning stations or go deeper! So bump up the ISO and take some nice natural-light shots.

The Famous Threshers

There's one bit of marine behavior that can be seen at Monad Shoal that's become world famous – that undertaken at the thresher-shark cleaning station. First seen by Malapascua fishermen, early pioneer divers worked the shoal to find out if thresher sharks could be seen, and it turned out they actually clean on the seamount. This is about the only place in the world where they appear with any predictability and scientists have come to study them on more than one occasion. A patient and stationary diver can get very lucky by waiting at a deep cleaning station.

Threshers (Alopias pelagicus) grow to a maximum of 3.3m. With their long, sweeping tails (which may make up 50% of their body) and bulbous bodies, they are easy to differentiate from other species. As with other members of the mackerel shark family, threshers give birth to live pups, usually between two and four at a time. Interestingly, researchers have recorded a form of intrauterine cannibalism among threshers, where pups in the womb attack and eat their siblings before birth.

The threshers are not seen schooling at Monad Shoal, but are usually solitary. They sometimes circle the cleaning station in twos and threes, but they arrive and leave separately. They are a wary shark. Although not generally regarded as a threat to man, divers should not get too close as it could interrupt their cleaning behavior, and they are easily scared. They will just swim away.

Divers rise before sunrise and make it to the site at first light. Then the waiting game begins. Although shy, the threshers will come close if curious or if they don't feel threatened. So occasionally look overhead and even behind as one might be closer than you think!

Also, when in the area, keep an eye out between dives – threshers actually leap from the water in breaches like dolphins or humpback whales. Few sharks do this. You might also see them slap the water with their big tails when trying to hunt and herd up schooling fish.

A rotating schedule has also been implemented for the dive shops so they are not all on the shoal at the same time. Shark sightings are pretty consistent if you leave at any time before 7am – you do not have to be the first boat there.

So, good luck! There have been some nice photos of these sharks taken, but hats off to those photographers because it isn't easy. You just have to hope the water is clear, it's sunny enough, you are in focus and the shark comes close.

The thresher morning dive may be the only dive people do out here. To be frank, the cleaning station areas often just aren't that interesting, unless you like a few anemonefish and lots of moon wrasses – so if you don't see a thresher you may chalk this dive up to a non-repeat. However, manta rays have become a common sight and even a few molamolas (ocean sunfish) and mobulas have been seen. The manta dive is usually done in the afternoon. These are big, ocean-going pelagic mantas and are really impressive.

If the mantas or mobulas don't show up, it's back to watching a few clownfish. But it's worth trying both the manta and thresher shark dives a couple of times. You may get lucky with one or both, and the encounter can be quite special.

Moving away from the cleaning station area offers a few more options. While at the cleaning stations the currents normally aren't too bad, if you head to the face of the seamount currents get stronger coming up the face

Malapascua Mantas

In 2008, a revelation was made public by Dr Andrea Marshall, a specialist in manta rays. For many years, biologists have thought that mantas found worldwide were all the same species. After suspecting the existence of a second species, Marshall began studying other populations across the globe. Through genetic and morphological analysis she confirmed that there is indeed a second species of manta ray that exists across temperate, tropical and subtropical waters worldwide. The two species have mainly overlapping distributions, but their lifestyles differ greatly; one is migratory and the other is resident to particular areas along the coast.

Observers believe that the mantas seen at Monad Shoal are the large, ocean-going, migratory mantas. Other differences between the two species lie in the color, skin texture, reproductive biology and the presence of a nonfunctioning type of sting on the tail of one of the species.

The smaller, more commonly known manta rays reside in the same areas year-round, are often encountered at coral reefs in shallow water and are often found in social unity. They will share cleaning stations with other mantas.

Due to their residential nature they face a grave threat from unsustainable fisheries, as other manta rays (from other areas) will not replace a dwindling population, making their regional extinction a likely possibility.

Far less is known about the larger species of mantas, its behavior or migratory patterns, as it appears to be more migratory and elusive, shying away from divers rather than seeking interaction as its smaller cousin often does. They clean individually and are noticeably larger than their reef-dwelling cousins.

The discovery of two distinct species has huge implications for the conservation management and protection of these mysterious gentle giants. The larger, ocean wanderer, such as those most frequently seen off Monad and Kimud Shoals, knows no borders, making collaboration between countries on its protection essential.

Thanks to Andrea Marshall, PhD (www.giantfish.org)

Beautiful carved thresher sharks can be found on Malapascua Island

of the sunken island and the marine life increases significantly. Here you will see schools of bigeye jacks and batfish, schooling barracuda, tuna, schooling bannerfish, big sea fans, soft coral trees along the wall and lots more.

The shoal also attracts other pelagics, such as other species of shark including whitetips, hammerheads and slinky silvertips coming up from the cool depths. Hammerheads are seasonal. As if that weren't enough, whale sharks occasionally visit and sightings are becoming more frequent both here and at Gato Island.

This is a slightly more advanced dive site due to depths, a need to control breathing and buoyancy and occasional currents. Most divers will want to do several dives here, as there's a lot of territory to cover. Diving depths average between 25m and 30m. Obviously, this is a good site for technical divers who know what they're doing, but strong currents can cause problems, so care should be exercised on all dives.

Kimud Shoal (also known as Devil Ray Sunken Island) is nearby and is a fairly small shoal. Almost circular, it is possible to swim all the way around the edge in one dive. This has become known as a place that is becoming seasonally consistent for a school of 100 hammerheads between December and April.

The top of the island lies at 12m to 16m, and the steep sides drop off to more than 200m. It is near Monad Shoal, so thresher sharks, mantas and mobulas are seen often. Turtles are occasional visitors.

The top of the island has a lot of hard coral, and many excellent hiding spots for moray eels. The sides are covered in soft coral growth. Many species of shrimp can be found among the corals and several species of unusual nudibranchs. The east side is especially interesting for its rock formations and overhangs.

Because of the drop-off, at any point on the island there is the chance of seeing pelagics such as sharks, rays and tuna.

55 CALANGGAMAN

Location: *S of Kimud Shoal*
Depth: *10-130ft (3-40m)*
Access: *Boat*
Range: *All levels*

This is one of those picture-perfect postcard islands, found south of Kimud Shoal. The island has a beautiful sandy beach with a fingerlike sandbar that comes and goes with the tides and typhoons. Part of the island also has a rocky shore with big palm trees. It is a bird sanctuary – the local name literally means bird place. One can walk around the isle in less than an hour. There are a couple of fishing huts but no permanent residents here.

Since it sits out on its own, unprotected, it needs to be a calm day to venture out here but it's worth the trip. On a calm day it's about an hour's ride from Malapascua, and three dives can be done here to make a day of it. Bring lunch for a beach picnic between dives.

Snorkelers will like the picturesque inner lagoon and can make their way out to the gentle slope that falls off to wall. The attractively adorned wall holds red and gold gorgonians sea fans, as well as plentiful fish and macro life.

In the sandy areas, expect to see snake eels, stonefish and mating hammerhead nudibranchs in the turtle grasses. The reef holds oddities such as mushroom coral pipefish, ornate ghost pipefish and clown triggers. Sea turtles are also common here.

Since this is close to the other pelagic shoals, the wall may bring large marble rays and various sharks such as the threshers and whitetips. Even whale sharks have been seen cruising here a few times.

Spinner dolphins frequently ac-

company the boat on the way out and back, riding the bow wave. Once a pod of pilot whales was also seen.

Malapascua Wrecks

As well as the reefs, drop-offs, pelagics and great muck dives, Malapascua also offers both modern and WWII wrecks. Most of these war victims can be seen without much difficulty and have become great artificial reefs, attracting an array of marine life.

In addition to the dives outlined here, there is another famous war wreck at Malapascua but it's a technical dive only. The **Pioneer Wreck** sits north of the island in 140ft to 170ft (42m to 54m) and is in good shape. A gunboat, the guns are still pointing upward and can be seen on descent. This is deep and for mixed-gas techies on calm days only.

Soft corals cover the wrecks

56 | DONA MARILYN WRECK

Location: *NW of Gato Island*
Depth: *60-110ft (18-32m)*
Access: *Boat*
Range: *Advanced*

This is one of the more popular wrecks in the area, but it is in open sea northwest past Gato Island so conditions must be fairly calm to dive it. She is a passenger ferry that went down more than 20 years ago in a typhoon and is now covered in marine life. The *Dona Marilyn* is over 300ft long (100m) and held a lot of passengers. The sinking was a major disaster and many people lost their lives. It now lies on its starboard side at 105ft, amazingly intact.

The corals on the wreck provide a nice overswim at about 65ft, along the portside. The wreck is penetrable by qualified divers. Much of its cargo lies scattered over the sea floor, which is also home to nurse sharks and black-blotched rays. The portside of the wreck is festooned with purple and red soft corals. The ship's hull has become home to a wide variety of marine life. Look for resting marble rays in the sand and blue-spotted rays. Some whitetip sharks live under the bow. There is current flowing over the wreck most of the time that brings in eagle rays and even mobula devil rays in the water column.

Dive operators say the fish that live there grow to a large size. Several varieties of sweetlips grow bigger here than at other dive sites, and a giant moray eel is living in the wreck.

Since it's a large ship that has never been salvaged, there's plenty to see but it is best done by experienced divers.

57 LIGHTHOUSE WRECK & LIGHTHOUSE WEST

Location: *West side of Malapascua, 5mins by boat*
Depth: *18-32ft (5-9m)*
Access: *Boat*
Range: *Novice/snorkel*

This WWII Japanese landing craft is one of three known war wrecks in the area and is available for long dives and for snorkeling. It was sunk before it could land and went straight down with a load of cement that was destined to be used to solidify a land gun emplacement on the island – what appear to be rocks are actually the bags of cement.

The **Wreck** is mostly in shallow water and you'll find yourself bobbing around in 10ft to 15ft of water looking at the remnants of the hull, which has broken into two pieces. Fish and marine life like this artificial reef and lone yellow-tailed barracuda, hermit crabs, reef oc-

Sweetlips

topus, Marley's butterflyfish, striped pipefish, juvenile harlequin sweetlips and banded sea snakes are among the things you may see on a dive or snorkel here.

You can get a two-for-one deal by also swimming over to **Lighthouse West**, which is easily reached from the landing craft. Lighthouse West is known for its seahorses. Do this dive late in the afternoon. Not only will you see a lot of cleaning action but this is also the island's most popular mandarinfish dive. At dusk the mandarinfish males seek females to mate with – bring a light and you can do an evening to dusk into dark dive to watch their antics.

58 TAPILON WRECK

Location: *Tapilon Island*
Depth: *70-90ft (22-28m)*
Access: *Boat*
Range: *Intermediate*

This freighter hasn't been identified, but the wreck at Tapilon was hit by torpedoes and sunk in 90ft of water. It's broken up but is still recognizable as a big ship. The resulting scattered wreckage has created great habitat and the currents feed soft corals. It has become a barracuda haven with a large shoal living above the ship. Big marble rays also enjoy the ship, and scorpionfish can be found camouflaged along its deck and upper reaches.

Look for smaller creatures too, such as flatworms, nudibranchs, moray eels, cuttlefish and squid. Macrophotographers will want to look in the many fire urchins for zebra crabs (sometimes with eggs) and Coleman shrimp, which live in these creatures and make colorful photo subjects. Ornate ghost pipefish and frogfish are also seen on the wreck at times – they seem to come and go.

MACTAN & CEBU CITY

Hardly a tropical paradise when viewed from the air, Mactan – a large, unprepossessing, flat, rocky island with little abundant greenery – has a huge number of dive centers (more than 100 at the last count) catering to divers from around the world.

Both international and domestic flights land at the Mactan-Cebu International Airport. The abundant resorts – from relatively cheap, small developments to some impressive luxury properties – offer a wide range of accommodations. Somewhat spread out, the resorts are mostly on the island's eastern side, which has a fringing reef with an impressive wall dropping off along its length. Unfortunately, in many areas the reef has been badly affected by both typhoons and dynamite fishing.

Mactan has a few areas worth diving and is also the jumping-off point for many sites in the Visayas, several of which are less than an hour away by bangka boat. Most resorts and dive centers throughout Mactan offer dive

training, much of it Professional Association of Diving Instructors (PADI) oriented, but the prices tend to be higher here than in other parts of the country.

Cebu City, a short taxi ride across either of the two bridges spanning the channel that divides it from Mactan, has no dive sites, but several retail dive centers here supply equipment and services to the region's many dive operators and their customers.

Cebu's harbor is a convenient boarding point for live-aboard boats and fast ferries to outlying islands, and its north and south bus stations see a steady stream of divers making pilgrimages to Sogod (home to Alegre Beach Resort and some fair diving) and points north,

Mactan & Cebu City Dive Sites	GOOD SNORKELING	NOVICE	INTERMEDIATE	ADVANCED
59 TAMBULI FISH FEEDING STATION	●	●	●	●
60 KON TIKI HOUSE REEF	●	●	●	●
61 MARIGONDON CAVE	●	●	●	●

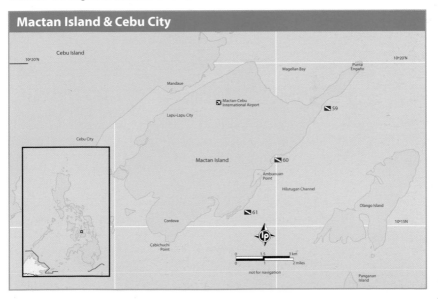

Mactan Island & Cebu City

Mandarinfish are sought-after photo subjects

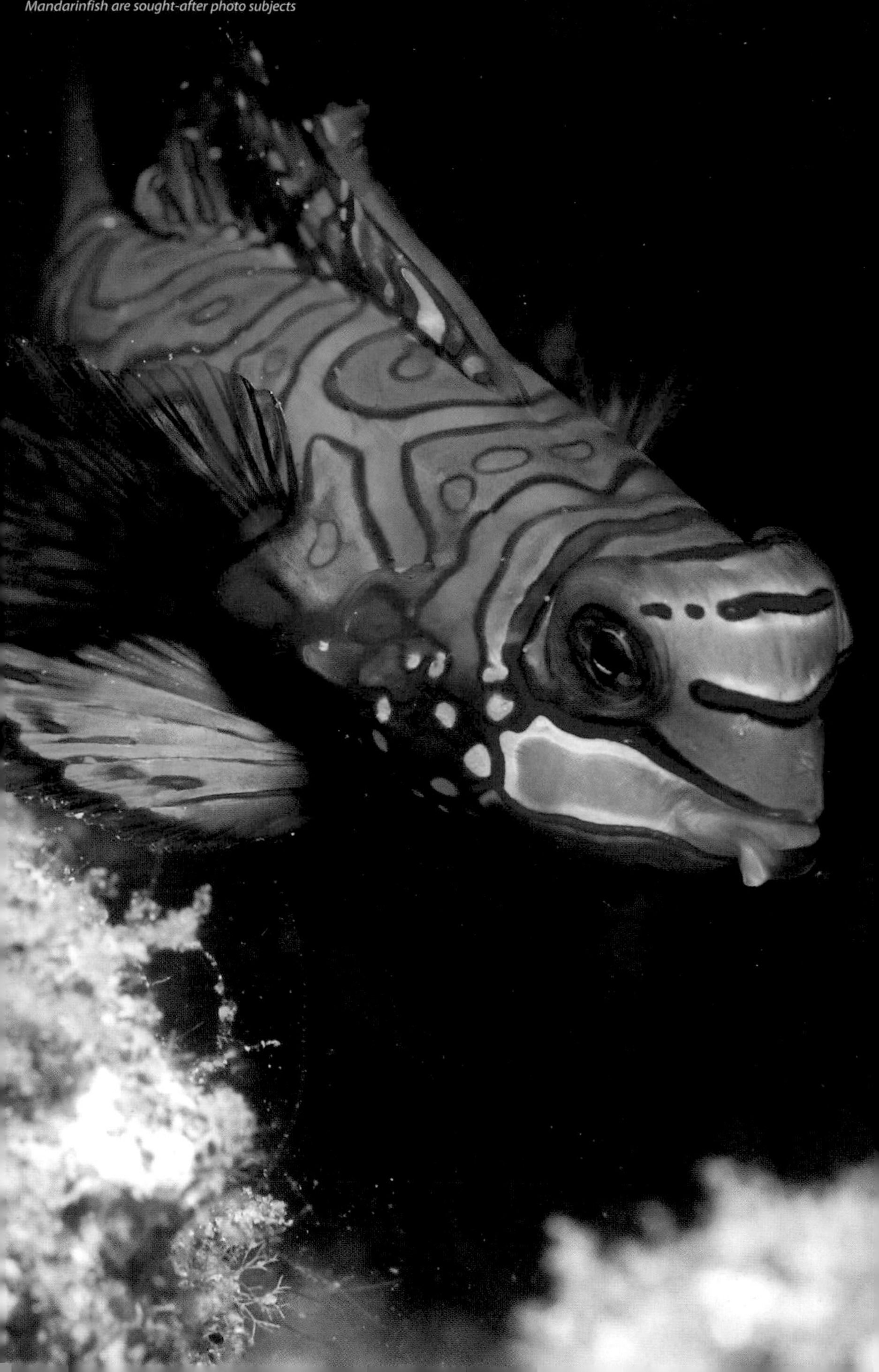

as well as to Moalboal, on the southwest coast of Cebu Island.

On your deco day, the Mactan Island Aquarium is available for you and the kids.

59 | TAMBULI FISH FEEDING STATION

Location: *Off Tambuli Beach Club*
Depth: *0-100ft (0-30m)*
Access: *Shore or boat*
Range: *Novice*

A popular training site and a good orientation to local dive conditions, Tambuli Beach Club is a comfortable and long-established dive resort at the northeastern end of Mactan. The beach has the trademark white sand and divers can walk into a swarm of fish. This is a good place for underwater photographers to shoot the local inhabitants up close.

There's a sea grass sand plain with a scattering of small coral heads that becomes lusher at around 45ft. It gets steeper here and drops off to about 80ft, forming a miniwall. For more-experienced divers, an unusual artificial reef lies in-between at 65ft: Tambuli Beach Club has anchored an old twin-engine Bonanza aircraft to the sea bottom. It is now home to a variety of marine animals and is quickly being covered by small hard and soft corals and barnacles. To permit easy penetration, the doors were removed, as were the propellers, most of the wings and the avionics. Pufferfish, porcupinefish, brown tangs, groupers and surgeonfish have taken up residence in the plane, and an occasional eagle ray sometimes passes by.

Surrounding the site are many anemones and clownfish, bubble corals with commensal shrimp and sometimes orangutan crabs, sea pens and triggerfish. Steer clear if mature triggerfish

are nesting. Sea moths, ghost pipefish, sea snakes, lionfish and stonefish are also well represented, mostly in the sea grasses. Watch out for the stinging hydroids that are liberally festooned around the area.

Another annoying factor to consider is the large amount of water traffic, including many bangka boats and jet skiers – some of whom seem to love nothing more than to use a diver's safety buoy as a marker to race around. Listen carefully for the sound of motors before ascending to the surface.

60 | KON TIKI HOUSE REEF

Location: *Kon Tiki Resort*
Depth: *10-100ft (3-30m)*
Access: *Shore*
Range: *Novice*

Red gorgonian fans near reeftop

Spiny sea urchin

Although it's possible to dive beyond 100ft (30m) here, it's not necessary. This is a fairly easy dive and is used as a training ground by many instructors teaching on Mactan. Unlike most of the reef dives along this extensive reef system, the Kon Tiki House Reef is actually alive and flourishing.

Kon Tiki Beach Hotel is a dedicated budget dive resort that was one of the first properties developed along the coast. The owners have zealously guarded the reef, which starts right off the seawall (there is no beach here, only a few rocks). Their efforts have paid off. The Kon Tiki House Reef is a showpiece that attracts divers from all over the island. It's unlike the rest of the Mactan coast, where the once-impressive fringing reef has seen significant destruction through illegal fishing, coral collection and environmental neglect.

The top of the reef is covered in boulders, coral bommies and small sandy patches, sloping gently to the lip of the wall a few meters offshore. The wall then plummets irregularly down into the depths of the Hilutugan Channel, the seemingly bottomless body of water that separates Mactan from nearby Olango Island. As a result, despite the usual lack of strong currents, these waters are often visited by large pelagics, including occasional whale sharks.

The Kon Tiki Wall is one of the better areas to spot pelagics, but even if they don't show up, the reef itself is worth the visit. It's covered in big gorgonians, sea whips and fans, sea stars, feather stars and crinoids; lots of colorful soft and hard corals cover every part of it. The ledges, cracks and crevices are home to a variety of crustaceans and plenty of reef fish, such as snappers, groupers, angelfish, parrotfish, gobies and wrasses. Tuna, barracuda and jacks are often spotted finning by, and larger pelagics are likely visitors. Worth more than one dive, the Kon Tiki House Reef stands as proof that dive resorts can, and should, make a difference in protecting the underwater environment.

The dive shop at the resort now offers tech diving here, as the wall continues down past 160ft (50m).

61 | MARIGONDON CAVE

Location: *E of Marigondon*
Depth: *16-130ft (5-40m)*
Access: *Boat*
Range: *Intermediate*

Marigondon Cave is a particularly impressive dive at the southern part of Marigondon Reef. Nitrox is recommended for this dive as most of it is deep. Currents can be strong along the wall that leads to the cave, but once inside, it is normally still and clear. You can reach the wide cave entrance by descending the wall to around 95ft (28m). The bottom of the cave is at around 130ft (40m) (the cave itself slopes slightly downward from the large entrance before rising up again), so watch your depth. The cave is massive, stretching back for almost 145ft (45m), the floor and ceiling rising as you move farther in.

At the far end of the cave is a tiny aperture (just large enough to get your head into) that opens to a small subterranean grotto. At first glance it's pitch black, but as you become accustomed to the dark, you'll notice dozens of pairs of 'eyes' winking at you in the darkness. These are the bioluminescent patches on the faces of dozens of flashlight fish, a species that made this amazing adaptation to survive in dark interiors.

The inside also has sea fans, sponges, lionfish and a memorial to a diver who wasn't watching his time and depth.

Remember to watch your bottom time in this cave, as you will have to descend several meters again to get out of the entrance, and you don't want to incur a decompression penalty by overstaying in the shallower interior. The reeftop is a good place to do a safety stop, as it is relatively shallow, with coral heads and some skittish fish around.

Spinecheek clownfish

MOALBOAL

Moalboal, whose name means 'bubbling water,' a reference to some nearby freshwater springs, is a quiet, peaceful little village that has become a mecca for divers. To get here from Cebu City you must cross the mountainous spine of skinny Cebu Island. Arrange for a clean and quiet private car and driver or negotiate a taxi ride. Your hotel or dive shop can set this all up in advance so you can be met at the airport.

Ahead of its time, Moalboal started to attract divers in the late 1970s. Then, it was a backpackers' paradise. A dive cost less than US$5 and a training course (of sorts) not much more. Times have changed: Moalboal is now an internationally recognized center of diving excellence, with more than a dozen high-quality dive centers teaching reasonably priced courses to all levels of divers. Several local operators offer Nitrox and technical dive training. Another indication of the local dive operators' professionalism is that every local dive site now has a mooring buoy.

Aside from visiting local sites, Moalboal dive centers organize dive safaris to many other parts of the Visayas, including the reasonably close Apo Island.

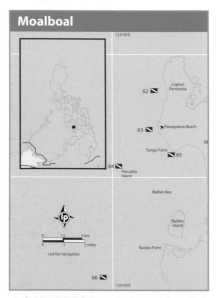

Moalboal

Moalboal Dive Sites	GOOD SNORKELING	NOVICE	INTERMEDIATE	ADVANCED
62 COPTON POINT	•	•		
63 PANAGSAMA BEACH (HOUSE REEF)	•		•	
64 PESCADOR ISLAND	•		•	
65 TONGO POINT	•		•	
66 SUNKEN ISLAND 1	•		•	

Diver inspects a crinoid

A sea urchin clingfish

62	COPTON POINT

Location: *West Copton Peninsula*
Depth: *0-130ft (0-40m)*
Access: *Shore or Boat*
Range: *Intermediate*

Strong, unpredictable currents may pass through here, but the diving is reliably good. It is possible to make a beach entry (snorkelers often do) but divers tend to get here by boat. The top of the reef is sandy and home to plenty of hard and soft corals (including some lovely staghorn and sea whips), as well as sponges. Watch out for the sea urchins! There are blue-spotted rays in the sand and you'll see plenty of anemones billowing in the current.

At the northern end of the reef the wall starts at around 5m, making it ideal for snorkelers. The bottom slopes steeply away to the south, and the lip of the wall deepens to around 23m at the southern end. As the current is usually south to north, this makes for an intelligent 'deeper first' section and a perfect safety stop on the shallower, prolific northern end of the reef. The wall itself has some fair-sized sea fans and gorgonians on it.

Fish you might expect to find include almost anything you can think of. Several species of triggerfish and angelfish abound, some stunning chromis and anthias lurk in the table corals, and sea snakes hunt here, morays too. Garfish, pipefish, puffers, snappers, groupers (some large individuals are deeper down the wall), fusiliers and Napoleon wrasses all call this area home.

63	PANAGSAMA BEACH (HOUSE REEF)

Location: *Off Panagsama Beach*
Depth: *0-130ft (0-40m)*
Access: *Shore or boat*
Range: *Novice*

This site is as good as or better than many of the region's other shallow snorkeling and diving sites. The reef is a popular training ground, and its shore accessibility allows dive centers to pass the transportation savings to their customers. The wall stretches quite a way along the coast. Divers and snorkelers may enter from several areas between Panagsama and Bas Diot (just out from Moalboal Reef Club).

Take a flashlight to explore the various small caves along the wall. The wall, which drops down in stages to more than 40m, is still impressive in many places, with gorgonians and plenty of hard and soft corals. Morays and sometimes sea snakes prowl this area, and you'll see lots of species of crinoids.

A shoal of bigeye trevallies is stationed around Moalboal pier's barnacle-encrusted legs, and you can study plenty of small fish and fry on the reeftop. Deeper down the wall, you may encounter catfish, some snappers, gobies, angelfish, chromis and anthias, morays, anemones and clownfish. Whale sharks have been seen here in recent years so keep an eye on the blue.

Red whip corals along a wall

64 PESCADOR ISLAND

Location: *W of Panagsama Beach*
Depth: *0-130ft (0-40m)*
Access: *Boat*
Range: *Novice/intermediate*

It was Pescador that put Moalboal on the diver's map and Pescador that remains its biggest draw today. The uninhabited island is the most obvious landmark off the coast of Moalboal: you can see it from just about anywhere along Panagsama Beach. An almost constant stream of dive bangkas make their way back and forth from Moalboal to Pescador, carrying load after load of happy divers.

Local dive operators have placed mooring buoys at several locations around the island to protect the reef from anchor damage. It's possible to swim around the entire island in one dive, but Pescador deserves several dives to be fully appreciated.

Currents are strong, but the visibility is frequently great. Snorkelers can swim over the shallower sections of the reef, which range from around 10ft to 30ft to the wall. There is plenty to see, but watch out for bangka traffic and the current.

Pescador has everything you'd want and expect of a tropical reef dive. For many years its gorgonians and fan corals set the standard by which other Philippines dive sites were judged. Another of its claims to fame are the Spanish dancers, a species of large nudibranchs that wiggle and shimmy their way across the reef.

The top of the reef is festooned with many kinds of corals, including staghorns and sea whips, table and boulder corals. Deeper down the wall you'll see lots of tube and basket sponges and plenty of colorful, well-developed soft corals all over the place, as well as some fair-sized clumps of black coral. The vertical wall boasts some impressive overhangs and crevices. The wall's north face reaches below 160ft (50m), so watch your depth.

Fish life encompasses virtually every tropical-reef species you can imagine. Prevalent species include scorpionfish, sea snakes and moray eels. Mantas and sharks are occasionally seen, and some

very lucky divers have spotted whale sharks. Reef species include anthias, gobies, lizardfish, groupers, snappers, rabbitfish, tuna, barracuda, turtles, parrotfish, Napoleon wrasses – you name it, it's probably here.

One of the most-popular areas of Pescador is the **Cathedral**, a stunning crevice that descends to 110ft (34m). At around noon, shafts of light dapple the corals and illuminate the interior in an ethereal light show. You can also look for another smaller cave, known as **Lionfish Cave**, and some large boulders as well.

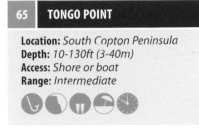

65	TONGO POINT

Location: *South Copton Peninsula*
Depth: *10-130ft (3-40m)*
Access: *Shore or boat*
Range: *Intermediate*

Tongo Point is a good site year-round, though currents are sometimes strong and unpredictable. It can be best during *amihan* (the northeast monsoon) from November to February. This brings very clear water to the site although the seas may be a bit rough. Snorkelers who don't mind a long swim can access this area from the beach, but divers will most likely arrive and depart by boat.

Though you won't see a lot of fish here, the corals are truly exceptional, especially the sea fans along the wall. Some healthy soft corals grow here too. Reasonably sized groupers often hang out along the wall below 100ft (30m).

At the north end of the point, snorkelers can explore impressive shallow coral archways. At the south end, just off the reef, some really healthy coral formations are also worth checking out.

Red fans and diver

66 SUNKEN ISLAND 1

Location: *SW of Badian Point*
Depth: *82-130ft (25-40m)*
Access: *Boat*
Range: *Advanced*

Strong currents and an open-ocean free descent to 80ft (25m) are the hallmarks of this remarkable seamount. Obviously, only advanced divers escorted by a knowledgeable dive guide need apply. The mount is covered by healthy hard and soft corals and some impressive sponges, especially barrels, as well as the ubiquitous gorgonians, which are especially grand here. Mantas occasionally pass by this site, and it's common to see plenty of pelagics, such as tuna, mackerel and barracuda.

Grey reef sharks are sometimes spotted, and you'll certainly see some very large lionfish. The funny looking frogfish (anglerfish), a rarity in most places, is quite common here, as are triggerfish, Napoleon wrasses, surgeons, pufferfish, groupers, snappers, sea snakes, angelfish – in fact, most species you would expect to find on a current-swept seamount in the Visayas – are well represented.

DUMAGUETE

Dumaguete sits in the shadow of the impressive dormant volcano Mt Talinis. Dumaguete City is the lively capital of the Oriental Negros province on Negros Island. It's a university town on the east coast facing southern Cebu; dubbed 'the center of learning of the southern Philippines,' it has seven universities and colleges. This means there's a lot going on intellectually and socially.

Dumaguete can be reached by fast ferry boat from Cebu, although they sometimes cancel without notice. It is more reliably served daily by domestic-airline flights from Manila and almost daily from Cebu City. The flights take less than an hour from either hub; the jet ferry takes about four hours out of Cebu City with one stop. The city has jeepneys and pedicabs to get you around. Arrange with your hotel or dive shop for pick-up at the airport as many resorts are outside of town.

In town, be sure to see the Dumaguete Belfry, which is one of the oldest landmarks and sits net to the grand St Catherine of Alexandria Cathedral. Dumaguete is a great town to take a stroll. Silliman University has a wonder-

Finger corals

Dumaguete Dive Sites		GOOD SNORKELING	NOVICE	INTERMEDIATE	ADVANCED
67	TACOT	•	•		
68	CALONG CALONG	•		•	
69	DUCOMI PIER	•		•	
70	SAN MIGUEL POINT	•		•	
71	BANCA WRECK & CAR WRECK	•		•	
72	POBLACION DAUIN	•		•	
73	MASAPLOD NORTE MARINE SANCTUARY	•		•	
74	MASAPLOD SUR MARINE SANCTUARY	•	•		
75	BAHURA HOUSE REEF (PANABOLON REEF)/MANDARIN POINT			•	
76	APO ISLAND	•		•	

ful campus, with over 300 acacia trees, and the night market along Rizal Blvd offers great stands with grilled fish and sea specialties. The general nightlife on Rizal Blvd is also fun and great for walking around and enjoying the ocean air.

With some cozy beach resorts about an hour or less down the road at Dauin, the Dumaguete region is becoming popular with divers from around the world. It's an interesting area. The Dauinanon (people residing in Dauin)

use a Cebuano dialect, however, they have a certain diction that makes them unique from others who use this dialect. There are indigenous people in the town of Baslay high in the mountains. Dauin originated from the word 'dwende' or dwarfs; they say that there used to be a lot of mischievous dwarfs residing here – this may be why the muck diving for small stuff is so good.

Several nice boutique resorts now feature dive services or are dedicated

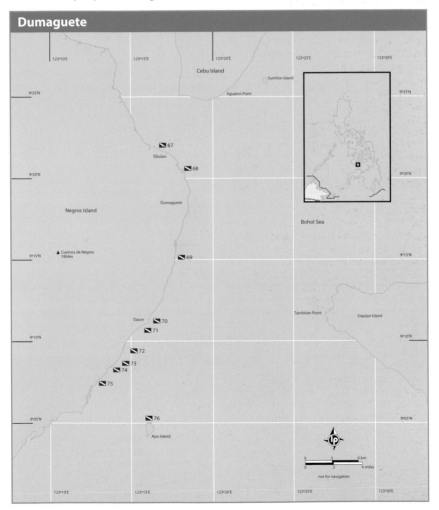

Green sea turtle descends to the reef

67 TACOT

Location: *N of Dumaguete City, offshore of Sibulan*
Depth: *40-75ft (12-23m)*
Access: *Boat*
Range: *Advanced*

dive resorts. Many have spas. Many also have protected house reefs, and a number of reserves and preserves are popping up along the coast. The importance of diving is even overshadowing tourism and the reserves are well patrolled. However, you can always tell where the boundary ends as there will be big bamboo fish traps just outside the conservation areas, with rocks and ropes draped over corals and sponges with no regard to the health of the reef even though food fish are pretty much gone along this coast and all you seem to see in the huge traps are tiny anthias and butterflyfish. The fish life within the conservation areas is much better as the fish seem to know where it's safe.

The most popular dive area here (and one of the better sites in the country) is Apo Island. It is a conservation success story and divers should go, spend the day, make three dives and tour the island. There are even a couple of small dive resorts there. It is maybe 1½ to two hours by boat from Dumaguete but only about 30 to 45 minutes out of Dauin. In all, there are at least 60 known dive sites between Sibulan, Dumaguete City, Dauin and Apo Island.

This underwater seamount often attracts large pelagics, usually has great visibility and always has strong currents. It is not a dive for amateurs. You'll drop off the boat into blue water and follow the anchor line down, or free swim, to the top of the underwater mountain. When a current is running, you'll know how it feels to be a flag on a pole on a windy day, and there's no time to clear ears and futz around.

The reef itself is surrounded by a fair selection of fish life (groupers, snappers, puffers, parrotfish and angelfish, among others), and the corals are healthy and large as a consequence of the nutrient-filled currents. Gorgonians, pretty soft corals and some reasonable outcroppings of table, brain and boulder corals decorate the seamount.

As the dive is relatively shallow, most divers will have enough air to explore the reef quite thoroughly, especially if you do two dives here. Do watch your bottom time to avoid a decompression penalty, as this is not a good spot to hang out.

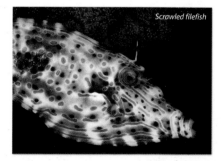
Scrawled filefish

Location: *N of Dumaguete*
Depth: *10-120ft (3-36m)*
Access: *Boat*
Range: *Novice–intermediate*

Location: *Ocean side of the Ducomi Plant, Bacong Town*
Depth: *3-90ft (1-27m)*
Access: *Boat*
Range: *Intermediate*

There are three dive sites along this reef. The wall starts at roughly 45ft and drops down to a good 120ft, although most of the diving is done in the 60ft range. There is a nice topography for divers to follow, but watch your depth gauge as the water can be clear and the rolling terrain deceptive. At one point the wall cuts back and forms a sheer drop.

There is a large curve in the wall with small coral outcrops, and on top of the wall you will find large rope sponges and lots of small anemones. The site can easily be called spiny-lobster paradise. There are big, reclusive crabs and spotted eels. Look into the blue water and you may see some spotted eagle rays.

Healthy table corals

Ducomi Pier is part of Bacong Town, the next town after Dauin going north. This is like going to Truk Lagoon and diving on the coral-laden masts of the ships there, except there are many, many masts. It's a dazzling maze of color and marine growth that always warrants a couple of dives. It is actually the Dumaguete Coco Oil Mill Pier and if there are big ships in, there is no diving. Even without a ship, divers must schedule their dives and be on time as there are likely other shops scheduled right behind.

The pier is huge and underneath are dozens of supporting pillars that have been washed by offshore currents and as a result, have years of beautiful coral growth on them. They are home to fish schools, many small fish and lots of odd invertebrates. Near the main pier there is also a smaller, free-standing mooring with many pillars as well.

The pier underwent renovation and strengthening in 2009 and some of the dense coral, encrusting sponge and marine growth was stripped for this work. Local dive shops worked with the company to minimize the damage but some of the pillar bases and a few of the pillars themselves had to be stripped to complete the job.

Still, it's an amazing dive into a coral wonderland with lots of light changes, different places for sun rays to pop through and hiding place after hiding place for creatures such as frogfish, lionfish, seahorses, crabs and shrimps. And as a bonus, the sandy area north of the pier where the dive boats stay is

A cuttlefish camouflages itself as a crinoid

also great for muck, with a sandy bottom and some sea grasses up shallow. You can do one dive wide angle and the next macro and come away with some very nice images.

Head down the sandy slope and swim out to the free-standing mooring. This is a deep anchorage so you can work your way down to 70ft or 80ft, but the bases of this pier were stripped for the renovation work, so there's more to see in the 30ft to 60ft range. Look at the many soft corals, gorgonians and small cardinalfish hiding in black coral trees. Then make your way across to the main pier.

Here you will see a maze that has a surprise around every corner. Aside from even more large, red gorgonians and big soft corals, there are big ball, rope and encrusting sponges and hard-coral growth. Fusiliers and porkfish course in and out, and there's a huge school of silver moonies. This place can be mesmerizing – remember to keep an eye on air and depth. At the dive's end you can make the swim back to the boat and a deco stop in the sea grasses where you will see sand anemones and saddleback anemonefish.

On your second dive get your macro eyes on. Even in the sand on your swim to the pier there will be lots to see. Don't overlook small pieces of junk and fallen trees – they hold tiny frogfish. There are some very large watchdog gobies, with stunning large bulldozer shrimp keeping their holes clean. Pygmy cuttlefish, ornate ghost pipefish and some cryptic nudibranchs can all be seen in this mucky area.

On the piers, especially the main pier, you will see (normally with the help of your eagle-eye guide) camouflaged frogfish. Look for Chromodoris nudibranchs moving along the sponges. Seahorses hide among the corals; look down to the sea floor for cockatoo waspfish. Also, watch where you put your hands as the scorpionfish here are plentiful, in varied sizes and very well-camouflaged. Also, prickly leather jackets and filefish like this habitat, which aids in their camouflage. After the dive, check out the sea grasses again for your last macro fix. This is one of the strangest and more-colorful dives you can do in the Philippines and it should not be missed.

Juvenile lionfish

70	SAN MIGUEL POINT

Location: *North Dauin*
Depth: *15-82ft (5-25m)*
Expertise: *Novice*
Access: *Boat*

Sand, sand and more sand! This buoy-ed sanctuary has corals scattered across the sand, but is mainly a macro heaven containing seahorses, frogfish, octopus, bobtail squid and pygmy cuttlefish.

Most of the diving around the corals is in the 30ft to 60ft range while the sand is both deep and shallow.

Take a good guide as oddities such as devil scorpionfish *(Inimicus)*, harlequin and ornate ghost pipefish, twin-eye goby, double-spot lionfish, flasher scorpionfish, blue-ringed octopus and Spanish dancers (you can often see the egg ribbons) can all be found here.

71	BANCA WRECK & CAR WRECK

Location: *North Dauin*
Depth: *15-100ft (5-30m)*
Expertise: *Novice/intermediate*
Access: *Boat*

Two sites sit pretty much side by side here and are great for seeing the many odd and unusual critters that this area has to offer. **Banca Wreck** is a sandy plain leading to a slope. Down the slope at 70ft to 80ft are the remnants of a large bangka boat. It's starting to fall apart but that doesn't keep it from being a great artificial reef and lots of critters have been attracted to it.

Nearby is also an artificial reef of old tires. You'll find these kind of artificial reefs at many Dumaguete dive sites as they have been part of university-biology-student studies and conservation projects. There are hingebeak shrimp of all sizes found in this cleaning station. On the bangka, look for more cleaner shrimp – they will come out and clean your teeth if you offer them a chance! Juvenile sweetlips, angelfish, mantis shrimp and others can be seen here. Keep an eye out for stonefish and scorpionfish, which can be found in the sand and in the wreck.

Make your way back up the slope and you will find thorny seahorses, pygmy cuttlefish, harlequin ghost pipefish, beautiful male elegant sand divers, roaming nudibranchs, juvenile lionfish and lots more. The shallows have sea grasses good for even more small stuff; look out for the possibility of a mimic octopus that has been seen in this area.

The **Car Wreck** site actually adjoins the Banca Wreck. Go down to 90ft (27m), where there are the wrecks of two cars that are now encrusted in marine life. Look around to see what's living in the vehicles now.

Work your way back up the sandy slope catching all the macro action as you slowly fin up. There will be frogfish, flamboyant cuttlefish, pipefish, dwarf lionfish and plenty more. A good guide can make you feel silly here as they keep seeing things a normal diver tends to overlook. These are great critter dives.

---

72 POBLACION DAUIN

Location: *Poblacion Dauin*
Depth: *15-82ft (5-25m)*
Expertise: *Novice*
Access: *Boat or shore*

This is another one of the small, buoyed marine sanctuaries found along the coast and can be done as a shore dive or by boat. As the small sanctuaries go, it is actually one of the bigger ones and sometimes dives are split into an explo-

ration of east and west. But it can be done in a single dive.

Divers enter and find a sandy bottom to about 15ft. Then they are greeted by some amazing hard-coral cover that runs across the sanctuary and down past 75ft. Large fields of staghorn coral hold clouds of sapphire chromis, while big cabbage corals hold refuge for small puffers and the occasional scorpionfish.

Swim around and through the various formations looking at crinoids, rope sponges and sea anemones. These coral formations are great habitat for smaller fish. The variation in corals by depths here is also interesting to see.

Near the sandy area on the north is a pile of used tires that now serves as an artificial reef. Check the mouths of the cardinalfishes for eggs. There are also other juvenile fishes such as sweetlips here, as well as some sea grass that holds some interesting small creatures. You may see some razorfish flitting around.

Seahorse

Diver and giant frogfish

73	**MASAPLOD NORTE MARINE SANCTUARY**

Location: *North Dauin*
Depth: *15-82ft (5-25m)*
Expertise: *Novice*
Access: *Boat*

The Masaplod Marine Sanctuary is divided into two sections, Norte and Sur. They are not connected and have somewhat different terrain although you may see some of the same inhabitants.

The northern section of the sanctuary seems to be synonymous with blue-spotted stingrays. It is also home to a good variety of fish, which seem to have become accustomed to divers and make great photo subjects. A fish lens such as a 35mm or a good macro lens will keep you busy here.

Enter on the south and you can swim down a coral ridge to 70ft or just explore shallower. There's an open sandy area as you swim north with some interesting creatures in the sea grasses at 25ft. Deeper areas hold scattered coral heads. Look for such reef dwellers as double-ended pipefish, the blue-spotted stingrays, yellowtail snappers and even nudibranchs making their way across the sand.

Then as you swim further north you will see another large coral section that runs down the slope from 25ft to 50ft, as well as sweetlips and batfish, with even the chance to have bluestripe fusiliers and bigeye jacks swoop in. End the dive by swimming up into the sea grasses just outside the buoys where seahorses are often found.

This is a popular and fishy dive that is very productive for photography.

74 MASAPLOD SUR MARINE SANCTUARY

Location: *South Dauin*
Depth: *15-82ft (5-25m)*
Expertise: *Novice*
Access: *Boat*

A bit down the beach from Masaplod Norte is the Masaplod Sur Marine Sanctuary, which is also very fishy and is better known for its nice coral variety. Again enter here at the south buoy and head down the sandy slope to 30ft to 40ft.

Here the cover of table corals, staghorns and lots of other hard-coral formations is much more dense than the sanctuary's northern namesake and continues down past 80ft and far into the center of the sanctuary.

This dive is fishiest at the south end between 60ft and 80ft. Look around between the corals where lots of schools such as snapper, sweetlips, rabbitfish and others have taken residence in the valleys between the coral heads.

About three-quarters of the way across the sanctuary there is a sand plain and then some more coral cover at the end of the dive. Look for mantis shrimps, stargazers and thorny cowfish. Again exit outside the sanctuary buoys in the sea grasses. This is also a very good site for fish photos and macro.

A clownfish guards her eggs

Market Day

If you're staying in the Dauin or Zamboanguita you should set aside some time to visit the very busy, bustling market in Malatapay, a *baryo* (small town) in Zamboanguita. It comes alive with livestock, fruits, produce and just about everything under the sun starting Wednesday morning and running through the day.

Since this happens every Wednesday, local people often call it 'Malatapay Day'. There are also food stands and the local *lechon* (roasted whole pig) is cheap and legendary.

75 BAHURA HOUSE REEF (PANABOLON REEF)/MANDARIN POINT

Location: *In front of Bahura Resort and a bit south*
Depth: *15-82ft (5-25m)*
Access: *Shore or boat*
Expertise: *Novice*

This is a refreshing little reef in front of Bahura Resort & Spa. Also known as **Panabolon Reef**, it has lots of variation in terrain, bottom and coral cover. As it is a marine sanctuary, it cannot be dived at night so plan a day dive here. If you stay at the resort, it's an easy walk-in, but this can also be a boat or beach dive. If going from the beach, you head out over a sandy plain with short marine grass. The entrance is rocky only for a few steps on the smooth volcanic rocks.

Then corals begin to appear as the depth of around 20ft is maintained for quite a while. There are many healthy coral formations with lots of fish, such as spotted groupers, pompano and sweetlips. The different coral areas have nice table corals, big staghorn areas and some very odd lettuce and plating corals. It's a real smorgasbord, with lots of small chromis and anthias to add to the color and movement of the area.

The reef then slopes down, with scattered bommies that you should look in for all manner of small marine life. The crinoids have clingfish in their fronds that you can patiently try to photograph. There are some very photogenic sea anemones with bright purple tips and glowing purple bodies. Among the tentacles you'll find shrimp and Nemo. Look around at all the different anemones, then make your way back up to the shallows and look at the good fish variety here before ending your dive.

The south edge of this sanctuary has some coral rubble, and there are some nice corals outside the sanctuary as well. This is where **Mandarin Point** is found. Since you can't dive at night, divers start about 5pm or 5:30pm so they will be able to make a dive and then get back to the mandarins by dusk for the mating to begin.

The corals and sponges just outside the sanctuary are very nice and there is a huge, coco female frogfish that sits among the vase sponges in perfect camouflage. Fishermen seem to know where the sanctuary ends and you may see large bamboo fish traps tossed recklessly on the reefs with thick ropes going down the slope to anchor them. A look inside a trap often shows a few anthias and chromis that have wandered in – these certainly aren't food fish and the big fish have all taken up residence within the sanctuary, it seems.

Head back to the sanctuary and the coral rubble piles. It doesn't look like much but they hold beautiful nocturnal shrimp including tapestry shrimp, striped pipefish and mandarinfish. Keep your lights off them as they court. Once they move up into the water column to mate, you can try to snap their amorous actions as they are pre-occupied. But remember, when the sun sets you have to leave – there is no night diving allowed in the sanctuary.

The healthy Apo reefs have many anthias and lush corals

76	APO ISLAND

Location: *Off southeastern tip of Negros Island*
Depth: *10-115ft (3-35m)*
Access: *Boat*
Range: *Novice/intermediate*

This is one of the most famous dive sites in the Philippines and has been a well-cared-for marine sanctuary since 1982.

Apo is a volcanic island that juts out of the endless blue depths of the Tanon Strait trench. The channel between Dauin and the island is also an important migratory route for dolphins and pygmy sperm whales. In season marine-mammal tours are organized

by some dive shops to observe the five species of whales and six different dolphin species that have been sighted here. It takes between 45 minutes and an hour to get out here, less if leaving from south Dauin or Zamboanguita.

Apo Island is home to the first community-run marine sanctuary and it's one of the country's, and diving's, real success stories. Two small resorts are based on the island and day visitors also come to dive and snorkel. There are nine buoyed sites and a snorkel preserve.

The 72-hectare island has some very impressive rock formations scattered out into the sea, a small fishing village and an even smaller one, a protected marine reserve, fine-white-sand beaches and coves, some high cliffs, a lighthouse and diverse reefs. There are at least 650 documented fish species and 400 kinds of corals.

What's nice about the dives here is the great diversity of the coral. You can make a dive at Chapel Point, for instance, and experience hard corals similar to those found in Tubbataha. Then you go just halfway around the island to Mamsa and the speciation, fish life and terrain are completely different – more like that seen on Malapascua. Curiously, divers aren't allowed to wear gloves here. They should dive without fins, as these break all the coral. The island has some no-fishing areas, and a couple of no-diving areas. Conservation rules are enforced and there's a fee, usually covered through the dive shop, to use the sanctuary reefs.

Here is a brief look at the main sites: **Katipanan Point** (*katipanan* means shell) is generally blessed with just light currents and is protected most of the time. Sea turtles love it here and there are big elephant-ear blue sponges on the reef, too. In addition to its hard corals, **Chapel Point** has some stunning white-sand valleys and at dive's end a wall with a large cave at the end full of silvery baitfish. **Rock Point West** leads to a point atop a flat plain that sometimes attracts manta rays when there is current, while **Rock Point East** is situated at the island's eastern end with a large reef up top and a wall covered in coral that leads to another plateau. Very fishy. **Sanctuary Point** is a protected area and sometimes divers are not allowed here, to keep the area from feeling too much pressure. The dive has a photogenic area called Clown-

fish City. **Kan-uran Point** is named for one of the original inhabitants, by the name of Uran. This site has a deep wall, moderate current and lots of overhangs to find gobies in. Coral is diverse here as well. **Mamsa Point** is known for its huge school of bigeye jacks *(mamsa* means jackfish in Tagalog). The corals here are superb and the currents can be wicked but that makes the marine life interesting. Everything from tuna to frogfish might be found here and turtles definitely like this site. **Coconut Point** seems to always have currents and is a famous drift-diving spot. Sit in the deep sand channel to watch the fish life while ducking the currents. And at **Largahan Point** the sand is volcanic and the coral diversity quite high. Geothermal bubbles rise from the sand. Currents here are manageable.

If you have to choose a couple of dives, Katipanan or Chapel Point are both very easy and pretty dives with good marine life. Turtles seem to like the coral cover and maybe hydroids around Katipanan. For adrenaline, take Mamsa. When that big jack school appears out in the blue and you can get in the middle of them, it's pretty special. Plus bumphead parrotfish and Napoleon wrasses sometimes make the show. But the currents here can be pretty wild with strong down currents at times, so if your divemaster says it can't be done, try one of the Rock Point dives. That goes for a couple of the advanced reefs. Full-moon tides can put these sites off limits due to extremely strong current action.

Also make sure you go ashore here. The people are charming and the little village quaint and clean. It has a couple of small restaurants, or you can bring lunch to eat on the beach. If you follow the path through the village you will end up at the shore entrance to the sanctuary where you snorkel. There's also a hike up to a cliffside overlook of the site.

Apo History

The sanctuary program at Apo Island began in 1982 with the initiative of Silliman University Marine & Biology Department head Angel Alcala, PhD. It became a protected reserve under the National Integrated Protected Area Act under the jurisdiction of the Protected Area Management Board.

Liberty Pascobello, the former chief of the island, worked with Alcala in the initial endeavor and may be responsible for its success. The family tradition of protecting Apo Island exists today. Brothers Mario and Chester – the present-day Barangay Chief and the leader of the 'Bantay Dagat,' respectively – continue to sustain Apo Island for the next generation.

Nearby Sumilon Island was also part of the initial sanctuary experiment. But its leaders allowed dynamiters in and now most of the island's resources have been destroyed. Apo's leaders' vision is a true testament to marine conservation and has been recognized worldwide. Some 800 island residents benefit in some way from this unique sanctuary.

BOHOL

The lovely island of Bohol is another well-kept secret now getting out. A proud and independent people, Boholanos take care of the many natural wonders of their land. Welcoming and hospitable, the islanders have shown above-average interest in sustaining the environment, both above and below the waves.

The result has been an increase in visitors who are eager to experience the island's many natural wonders, as well as an improved infrastructure to accommodate and entertain them. Alona Beach on Panglao Island, which is connected by a causeway to the mainland and a few kilometers away from Bohol's sleepy capital of Tagbilaran, is the place where most divers will call home around the southwestern end.

Alona Beach is all about diving. Resorts – ranging from simple cottages and guesthouses for a few dollars a night to delightful medium-sized developments with adequate luxuries for a few dollars more – cater to divers; many well-equipped, professionally-run dive centers operate along the beach. Even the nightlife (what little there is of it) is geared toward the diving community. Hear tall tales of deep encounters at most restaurants and bars along the beach.

Bohol Dive Sites	GOOD SNORKELING	NOVICE	INTERMEDIATE	ADVANCED
77 CABILAO ISLAND		•	•	
78 NAPALING		•		•
79 TANGAN WALL		•		•
80 BALICASAG ISLAND		•		•

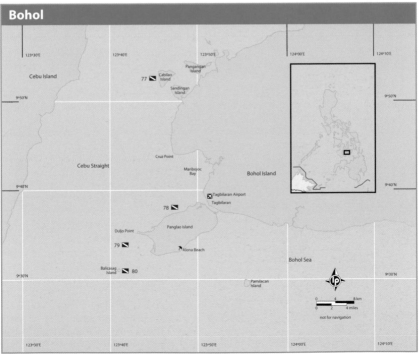

Alona Beach is a jumping-off point for dive safaris throughout the Visayas. Safaris are usually undertaken on larger bangka boats and often involve camping and barbecuing on remote islands during a two- to five-day trip.

The airport at Tagbilaran receives several flights daily from Manila and nearby Cebu, and every day several Super Cat ferries ply the route from Cebu's port for the one-way, 40-minute transfer. You can arrange in advance for transfers from Tagbilaran to Alona Beach through dive centers and resorts or private coaster (minivan).

77	CABILAO ISLAND

Location: *Off northwestern coast of Bohol*
Depth: *13-130ft (4-40m)*
Access: *Boat*
Range: *Intermediate*

This is where the famous scalloped hammerheads of Hammerhead Point congregate. This event happens about five months out of the year (December to April) but can be hampered by sea conditions, currents and depth. Dawn or dusk is when they are most likely to

Flying gurnard

appear so plan on rising early or dining late – it's worth the sacrifice.

This is not a novice dive and even intermediates will have to pay close attention to their guide to properly approach the school.

Cabilao, off the northwestern coast of Bohol, is an immensely popular dive area. This site can get quite crowded in season and, like all surrounding sites, is often afflicted with hellacious currents, though visibility is often excellent. If there are lots of dive boats around, it's obviously important to stick with your dive guide.

The reef off the point has many cracks, overhangs and coral gardens on it. It drops off to a ledge at 100ft (30m), and then drops again to much deeper water. This is a popular meeting point for the ubiquitous hammerheads, which shoal off the point in deeper water.

Hammerheads, despite their appearance, are actually extremely wary of human divers and tend to disperse to even deeper water if they feel provoked or threatened, such as by divers who approach too closely. Pay attention to the dive briefing and stick to the planned depths and times.

The reef itself is home to some reasonable gorgonians; large barrel sponges, whips, sponges and crinoids festoon the walls. Whitetip and grey sharks are frequently seen, and the pelagic menu is rounded out with barracuda, jacks, mackerel and tuna. Butterflyfish, Napoleon wrasses and triggerfish are common reef inhabitants, and you'll probably encounter fusiliers, Moorish idols, snappers and sweetlips.

Along southwest Cabilao, the strong currents provide for a perennial drift dive that often has better than 100ft (30m) of visibility. Though the drop-in point is a mundane section of shallow reef, the scenery improves as you drift either north or southeast.

The shallow southern portion of the reef is torn up from years of passing

Diver and spinecheek clownfish

typhoons – not much to see here but rubble and dead coral. Drifting north, you'll soon arrive at a wall that drops down to a ledge and then descends beyond the sport-diving limit. The wall is liberally covered with small gorgonians and sea fans, some impressive barrel sponges, baskets, lots of soft corals and sea whips and a clump or two of elephant-ear corals. Watch out for the abundant fire coral.

You'll see lots of sea stars around, as well as crinoids and many nudibranchs. Check out the colonies of ribbon and garden eels, as well as the small rays, on the sandy sections of the reef.

At the deeper end of the reef you'll find large groupers and Napoleon wrasses. The higher you go the more likely you'll encounter squirrelfish hiding in dark recesses, lots of soldierfish and fusiliers, some lionfish, snappers, sweetlips and damselfish, among others.

A southeasterly current will sweep you over the dead section of the reef to a wall that drops to more than 130ft (40m), again with similar features and marine life as that to the north, although the gorgonians are larger here, and you'll probably see some tube anemones. The major attractions on this dive are the impressive clumps of black coral along some of the deeper sections of the wall.

78 | NAPALING

Location: *NW Panglao Island*
Depth: *10-100ft (3-30m)*
Access: *Boat*
Range: *Intermediate*

This is a shallower dive with lots going on and some great places to snorkel. Though not the easiest site to get to when the weather is rough, this is nonetheless a great dive. Because of the frequent current, Napaling is often dived as a drift dive. The dive boats usually follow your bubbles and pick you up when you surface. Though it can also be dived from the adjacent beach, the current can make it difficult to get back to shore again.

The reeftop runs a fair distance and is quite shallow (about 8m deep) – excellent for snorkeling. Dynamite fishing has caused some damage, but aside from these areas the reef is relatively healthy, with some impressive table and pillar corals. Anemones, replete with the standard-issue clownfish, are quite prevalent here, and you'll probably find razorfish, damselfish, butterflyfish, parrotfish and a large shoal of anthias lurking about as well.

The wall and overhangs are quite impressive, covered with a good selection of hydroids, gorgonians, sponges and crinoids and lots of soft and *Tubastrea* corals. Whitetip sharks often make an appearance, and a good variety of nudibranchs and various worms pose for macrophotographers. Use a flashlight to see inside the wall's many holes – you'll likely be rewarded with glimpses of angelfish, morays and various crustaceans.

Clownfish in a purpletip anemone

79 | TANGAN WALL

Location: *Off Panglao Island*
Depth: *45-130ft (13-40m)*
Access: *Boat*
Range: *Intermediate*

This steep wall is pocked with lots of small caves and crevices that are home to some large groupers. The wall itself supports a number of fans and gorgonians that sprout from its steep sides, as well as a fair assortment of sponges, tunicates and soft and hard corals.

You may also spot wrasses, soldierfish and surgeonfish flitting about the coral growth, and an occasional barracuda swimming through the blue.

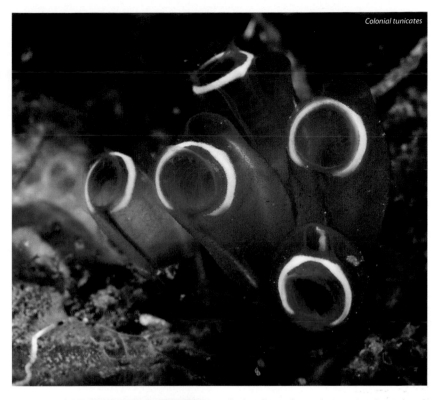
Colonial tunicates

80 | BALICASAG ISLAND

Location: *6km SW of Panglao Island*
Depth: *0-130ft (0-40m)*
Access: *Boat*
Range: *Intermediate*

About 6km from the southwest point of Panglao Island (45 minutes by bangka boat), Balicasag is one of the Visayas' best dive areas. Stunning corals, a great variety of fish life and visibility that often exceeds 120ft (35m) attract dive operators from around the Visayas. Unfortunately, as with other popular regions, this may mean that sites are crowded. Balicasag's marine-sanctuary status has helped it to flourish. Despite the volume of divers, neither marine-life species nor coral growth has diminished.

As with most reefs off Balicasag, **Southeast Wall** is festooned with a huge variety of corals, including table and star corals, sea whips, leather and soft corals. Anemones flourish, as do hydroids, sea stars, crinoids and sea cucumbers. In fact, this is one of the richest dive sites around, with nudibranchs competing for space with sea worms and shrimp. Fish life is prolific, with favorites such as the stunning tiny blue chromis, which live here in the fingers of huge table corals. You'll find fusiliers, Moorish idols, anthias, bannerfish, pennantfish, lionfish, jacks, snappers and wrasses, batfish and parrotfish. And that's just in the shallow sections of the reef.

The wall is garlanded with impressive gorgonians and sea fans; elephant-ear, barrel and basket sponges are everywhere; crinoids and various worms wiggle around all over the place. Several holes and crevices along the wall are home to soldierfish, squirrelfish and morays. Whitetip and grey reef sharks and barracuda cruise the wall frequently, and you may spot schools of rainbow runners and tuna on patrol as well.

Currents along the wall range from sluggish to 'OMG.' Try to find out which to expect before you get in the water, but be prepared for either. If you can head east, you'll eventually run into **Rudy's Rock**. It's similar to Southeast Wall, but with the added chance of spotting green turtles and a shoal of bigeye trevallies that are accustomed to divers.

Black Forest, along Balicasag's northeast shore, is another popular dive area. The reef itself is really more a sandy slope dropping away to well beyond safe sport-diving limits, so watch your depth. This can be another great site for techies, of course. Again,

currents can be quite vicious here and can head in almost any direction, so prepare for a drift dive accordingly. Obviously, an experienced local dive guide is a prerequisite for safe diving anywhere off Balicasag.

Massive clumps of black coral are the most significant feature of this site. You won't start to see the forest until you reach 100ft (30m). On the way down you'll pass many coral bommies, sea whips and small gorgonians sprouting out of the sand. Garden eels and moray eels are frequent neighbors here, sharing the waters with emperor and royal angelfish, Moorish idols, bannerfish, puffers, surgeonfish and a couple different types of triggerfish, among others. At the deeper sections of the reef, you may encounter some large skittish groupers, tuna, batfish and Napoleon wrasses. **Diver's Heaven** is also a popular site at the island.

Due to the depth of the black corals and the probable current, you should start your ascent with plenty of air left in your tank. Prepare to be washed off the reef into blue water during your safety stop if the current isn't cooperating.

Puffer hunting at a sea fan

SOUTHERN LEYTE

Southern Leyte (to the northeast of Cebu City) is a newer destination at Sogod Bay where local divers have researched and documented more than 20 excellent sites. Three dive centers operate in the area now, so adventurous divers looking for the epitome of pristine diving may well want to plan a trip here. The friendly locals, mostly into subsistence agriculture, lead simple lives in a very laid-back rural setting.

Southern Leyte is served by a fast Super Cat catamaran ferry that departs daily from Cebu Port for the 2½-hour trip to Maasin, the capital of Southern Leyte.

The best diving (and whale-shark sighting) season runs from November to May.

Southern Leyte Dive Sites	GOOD SNORKELING	NOVICE	INTERMEDIATE	ADVANCED
81 MAX CLIMAX WALL & BALUARTE	•	•		
82 TANGKAAN POINT	•		•	
83 NAPANTAW FISH SANCTUARY	•		•	
84 PETER'S MOUND	•		•	

81   MAX CLIMAX WALL & BALUARTE

Location: *Just off Lungsodaan, Padre Burgos*
Depth: *0 -130ft (0-40m)*
Access: *Shore or boat*
Range: *Intermediate*

Southern Leyte

Barrel sponges at reeftop

Max Climax Wall starts a few meters from shore, so it's possible to do a beach dive here. Divers usually arrive and depart by tricycle or pick-up – a new experience for most. The wall is riddled with cracks and crevices that are home to angelfish, snappers, Napoleon wrasses, sweetlips and groupers.

A little farther along the coast is **Baluarte**, which is very similar to Max Climax. Pelagics seen at both sites include jacks, tuna and barracuda. Sharks, turtles and eagle rays are also frequent visitors. Gorgonian fan corals are well represented at these sites, as are some black corals and soft corals. The reef is in very good condition. **Voltaire's Rock** is also a favorite here.

82	TANGKAAN POINT

Location: *Padre Burgos*
Depth: *0-130ft (0-40m)*
Access: *Shore or boat*
Range: *Intermediate*

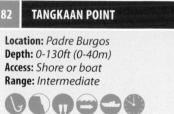

Divers have discovered several sites in and around Sogod Bay, and more are being found as the large reef systems are explored. The topography is diverse, with reef flats and walls interspersed with interesting limestone and rock formations. Much of the reef has been declared a fish sanctuary, and fishing is regulated by the local communities, so the corals and marine life thrive. Sogod Bay is a good place to see whale sharks, whales, dolphins, manta rays and several species of shark. Whale shark–watching cruises are a good option between dives.

Tangkaan Point, a half hour by road from Maasin, is a long land mass with some outstanding and varied pristine reefs and walls to explore just off the shore.

Snorkelers and divers will really enjoy much of the area, especially sites such as **Barrel Sponge Garden**, a small dropoff with massive barrel sponges, table corals and a huge variety of colorful hard corals. These sites are more easily accessed by boat, but locals can point snorkelers in the right direction to find the shallow coral gardens that characterize most of the area.

Turtle Rock is a site more suited for big-fish lovers. Green turtles are common here, as well as batfish, eagle rays and groupers. The corals are prolific and diverse, including gorgonians, tables, brain and sea whips, as well as sponges galore.

83	**NAPANTAW FISH SANCTUARY**

Location: *E of Middle Caye*
Depth: *33-130ft (10-40+m)*
Access: *Boat*
Range: *Intermediate*

This wall dive goes by many names, including Rio's Wall and Toshi's Wall. Of the many walls in southern Leyte, this one stands out – not only because of its huge gorgonians, black corals and soft corals, but also for its generally prolific

Sea-fan array

and colorful marine life. The corals, fed by the often-strong currents that sweep by, are especially healthy here. Reef inhabitants include batfish, groupers, sweetlips and pretty much every other reef fish you would expect to find on a thriving wall. Turtles and barracuda also frequent the area.

Take a flashlight to peer inside the cave, but watch your depth. If you don't locate it within the first few minutes of the dive, it's better to forget about it and avoid risking the bends. Just concentrate on the amazing reef life a little higher up the wall.

Local divers are setting up a mooring buoy to protect the reef from anchor damage at this increasingly popular dive site. A dive fee is being charged to help finance monitoring and protection measures undertaken by the Barangay Council of Napantaw.

84 PETER'S MOUND

Location: *Offshore Otikon, Libagon*
Depth: *33-130ft (10-40+m)*
Access: *Boat*
Range: *Advanced*

A seamount just 200m offshore, this is a fascinating site that serves as a cleaning station for large pelagics. To fully appreciate the experience, you should dive this site when a strong current is flowing.

For this reason, a boat is the preferred way to access the site. Be sure to descend and ascend using a shot line. The reef is abuzz with fish racing about and feeding, including Napoleon wrasses, groupers, sweetlips, surgeons, fusiliers, tuna and jacks.

Blue-spotted stingrays are common

Mindanao Dive Sites

One of the largest but poorest of the Philippines' 7107 islands, Mindanao has some great diving but a lackluster infrastructure. The island has a handful of luxury and dedicated dive resorts, but otherwise, in general, the accommodations and transportation options remain in the medium- to low-budget range.

Some parts of the province, especially the southwestern islands of Tawi-Tawi, Basilan Island and the Sulu Archipelago, have been hotbeds of piracy, kidnappings and assorted violence for centuries and still remain a virtual no-go for visitors. However, despite all the bad press and negative associations that the Abu Sayaf, MILF (Moro Islamic Liberation Front) and other extreme insurgent groups have created over the years, some parts of Mindanao – particularly Cagayan de Oro, Davao and General Santos and newly popular Siagao – have become popular with visitors. Mindanaoans of all religious and tribal persuasions are, in general, a welcoming and gracious people who make every effort to entertain and impress a foreign guest.

Divers will be happy to learn that some outstanding dive sites are within reach of the above-mentioned cities, and amenities are in place to facilitate hassle-free diving once you get there. In the diving areas you'll find good hotels and resorts at reasonable prices, a choice of dining and entertainment options and a law and order situation on a par with the rest of the country – attractive enticements for adventurers and tourists alike.

CAMIGUIN

Camiguin is a charming island off the coast of the Misamis Oriental province in northern Mindanao, just 55 miles (88km) from Cagayan de Oro. Although it's technically a part of Mindanao, divers often visit Camiguin on dive safaris organized from the divers' mecca of the Visayas, particularly from Alona Beach, Bohol, which isn't far away. Domestic flights arrive at Camiguin's rather quaint

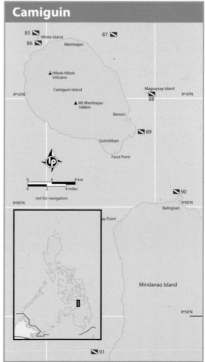

Camiguin Dive Sites	GOOD SNORKELING	NOVICE	INTERMEDIATE	ADVANCED
85 AGUTAYA REEF	•	•		
86 MEDINA UNDERWATER SPRINGS	•		•	
87 JIGDUP SHOAL	•		•	
88 PUNTA DIWATA	•		•	
89 CABUAN POINT		•		•
90 SIPAKA POINT		•		•
91 CONSTANCIA REEF		•		•

airport, but flights change and can be seasonal. Most take the ferry from the mainland.

Many small- to medium-sized resorts dot the island. All are reasonably priced, and most are attractive. A few dive services operate on the island, and Mantangale Alibuag Dive Resort on the mainland (close to Cagayan de Oro) also visits the island regularly.

85 AGUTAYA REEF

Location: *Off White Island*
Depth: *16-130ft (5-40m)*
Access: *Boat*
Range: *Intermediate*

With the towering bulk of Hibok-Hibok volcano watching over you from Camiguin Island, this idyllic sandy cay is a great place for snorkelers and divers alike.

The large, shallow Agutaya Reef has some healthy corals and lots of small reef fish darting around, and some larger specimens are holed up in the nooks and crannies of the corals and rocks. The eastern portion of the reef drops away from around 50ft. At this point you can explore a multitude of cracks, caverns and crevices that are home to a variety of larger fish such as barracuda, surgeons, tuna, eagle rays and sometimes sharks.

86 MEDINA UNDERWATER SPRINGS

Location: *Off White Island*
Depth: *20-108ft (6-33m)*
Access: *Boat*
Range: *Novice for the Aquarium, intermediate for Paradise Canyon*

You will find two dives here, both interesting and unusual, that feature cold freshwater springs (known locally as *alibuag*) bubbling out of the sea floor. These sites are both about 1000ft west of White Island's beach and are at the edge of the coral reef.

Descending to around 90ft, **Paradise Canyon's** walls are punctured with plenty of cracks and holes, home to a wide variety of marine life. Take a dive light with you and look for the cavern that you can enter and explore. A second dive in the area, known as the **Aquarium**, is (as the name implies) well endowed with corals and assorted marine life. This is an excellent training site and snorkeling spot, as it's relatively shallow.

A titan triggerfish hovers over its nest

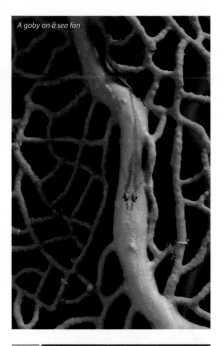
A goby on a sea fan

87 JIGDUP SHOAL

Location: *1.2 miles from Mambajao*
Depth: *0-130ft (0-40m)*
Access: *Boat*
Range: *Intermediate*

One of the best sites hereabouts, this shoal rises from the sea floor to form a sprawling reef more than 24 acres across. Teeming with all sorts of marine life, this reef is a wide-angle photographer's dream. Lush corals, excellent visibility year-round and a never-ending diorama of tropical reef fish, pelagics and macro-photography subjects make this a favorite repeat site for many divers.

Barracuda, tuna, several species of sharks and rays, wrasses, angelfish, surgeons, snappers and groupers are all likely candidates for observation. The current can be fierce at times, so be prepared to deal with it accordingly. If you have any doubts, turn around and head for the boat while your tank is still two-thirds full.

88 PUNTA DIWATA

Location: *Eastern tip of Gingoong Bay, Magsaysay Island*
Depth: *0-130ft (0-40m)*
Access: *Boat*
Range: *Intermediate*

The reef here has stepped ledges of coral that descend to the depths. The walls and overhangs are covered in sea fans, sponges and a variety of multi-colored gorgonians, sea whips and hard and soft corals.

Commonly seen species include groupers, sweetlips and snappers, while mantas are occasionally spotted. This is yet another excellent wide-angle site with usually good visibility unless it's been raining heavily.

An array of whip corals

89 | CABUAN POINT

Location: *Between Benoni and Guinsiliban Ports*
Depth: *0-100ft (0-30m)*
Access: *Shore or boat*
Range: *Novice*

A cuttlefish shows its tentacles

A delightful dive that's sure to attract the interest of wide-angle photographers, this site features stunning sea fans, branching corals and a huge variety of hard and soft corals and sponges.

You are sure to see angelfish, tangs, cuttlefish and parrotfish, and the usually light currents make diving here a breeze. Visibility ranges from 40ft to 115ft, depending on the recent weather conditions. This is a good training ground and ideal for snorkelers.

90 | SIPAKA POINT

Location: *Close to Mantangale Alibuag Dive Resort, Balingoan*
Depth: *0-82ft (0-25m)*
Access: *Boat*
Range: *Advanced*

A strong current can make this a wild ride, so the site is best suited for more-experienced divers. The currents bring nutrients, which in turn nourish the fantastic assortment of huge corals that abound here. Massive basket sponges, sea fans and table corals are common, together with a wide array of hard and soft corals, sponges and feather stars.

Look for stingrays hiding in the sandy spots, and groupers, snappers, wrasses, surgeons, parrotfish, angelfish and many other species darting in and out of the corals and rocks. Photographers will have a hard time deciding whether to use a macro or wide-angle lens – you'll probably have to make several dives at this spot to see its full potential.

91 | CONSTANCIA REEF

Location: *Offshore of north Balingasag*
Depth: *20-130ft (6-40 m)*
Access: *Shore or boat*
Range: *Intermediate*

Although some distance from shore, this tiny shoal with healthy corals on the south side is worth visiting because of the pelagic life you're likely to encounter. Eagle rays are quite common, and you may run into a turtle or two. Keep an eye out for the occasional manta. Tuna, jacks, barracuda, several species of sharks, rainbow runners and Spanish mackerel also frequent Constancia's tumbling walls.

On the reeftop, parrotfish spend much of their time resting and gathering above the lettuce corals, which cover much of the area. Sea fans and sponges proliferate, and a variety of reef fish, such as angelfish, wrasses, blennies, groupers, snappers and surgeonfish dart about between the coral cover. This is a good site for photographers, but the current can be a factor. Visibility is usually more than 82ft.

DAVAO

Davao is geographically the largest city in the Philippines. However, as with Puerto Princesa in Palawan, the published boundaries of the city don't reflect the demographics of the inhabitants. Much of the 'city' is sparsely inhabited farmland and forest. Despite apparent attempts to impose some form of grandeur on what is actually a pleasant provincial town, Davao retains a charm and appeal all its own.

Only a few degrees north of the equator, the Davao region enjoys a Hawaii-like weather pattern. It rains briefly most days, the hot sun shines almost every day and typhoons are unknown here (indeed, all of Mindanao is well south of the typhoon belt). Davao is a genuine year-round diving destination, something that is not lost on the local dive entrepreneurs, who visit sites around nearby Samal Island.

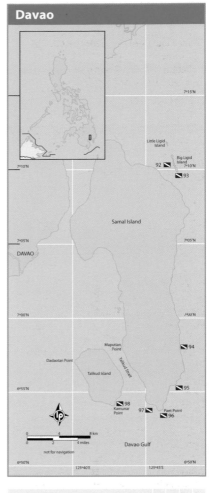

92 LIGID CAVES

Location: *Big Ligid Island, NE of Samal Island*
Depth: *0-100ft (0-30m)*
Access: *Boat*
Range: *Intermediate*

You can find the Ligid Caves by swimming over the leather-coral encrusted reef, past where the wall drops sharply from 52ft, then descending a several feet further until you reach the two cave systems.

One of the caves has three entrances that all lead to a central chamber filled with black corals, a variety of sponges and tunicates, soft corals and crustaceans such as sponge crabs. Around the caves' entrances you might see lionfish, scorpionfish, parrotfish and rabbitfish.

Davao Dive Sites	GOOD SNORKELING	NOVICE	INTERMEDIATE	ADVANCED
92 LIGID CAVES		•	•	
93 PINNACLE POINT		•		•
94 PINDAWON WALL		•		•
95 MUSHROOM ROCK		•		•
96 MARISSA 1, 2 & 3		•		•
97 MALIPANO JAPANESE WRECKS		•		•
98 LINOSUTAN CORAL GARDENS		•		•

Look for a large harp-shaped gorgonian and check out the resident razorfish, ideal subjects for a well-strobed photo shoot. Atop the reef, especially on night dives, look for the many golden sea cucumbers, hydroids and basket stars. This is also a fair snorkeling site for experienced snorkelers.

93 | PINNACLE POINT

Location: *Southeast tip of Big Ligid Island*
Depth: *26-115ft (8-35m)*
Access: *Boat*
Range: *Intermediate*

Red sea fan

Expect strong currents here – try to get in the water at high tide for the least current and best visibility. Head southeast along the wall, current permitting, taking in views of the gorgonians and fans. Check out the cracks and holes in the wall, where you can find bigeyes and cardinalfish. Some octopuses and morays also dwell in the smaller holes. Southeast of the point are three reef formations where schools of pennant butterflyfish, surgeonfish, jacks and several types of angelfish are frequent visitors. The center structure is covered in delightful pink soft corals, while the leeward side is festooned with large gorgonians, black coral and a host of anthias and *Tubastrea*.

Macro photographers will appreciate the many nudibranchs and similar subjects. Watch your depth on this dive, and make sure you have enough air left to get back to the boat's anchor line with enough time for a safety stop, which could be affected by strong currents.

94 | PINDAWON WALL

Location: *East side of Samal Island*
Depth: *33-115ft (10-40m)*
Access: *Boat*
Range: *Intermediate*

Pindawon is one of the better walls in the area, with some impressive overhangs and good hard-coral cover. Some spectacular table corals and black corals are features at this site, as well as major cabbage-coral colonies.

You may well run into some sea snakes, as the pickings are quite good for them. Some interesting nudibranchs live around the numerous crevices and cracks, and there is an average amount of fish life, including colorful harlequin shrimps and razorfish. You may also spot snappers and a few skittish groupers.

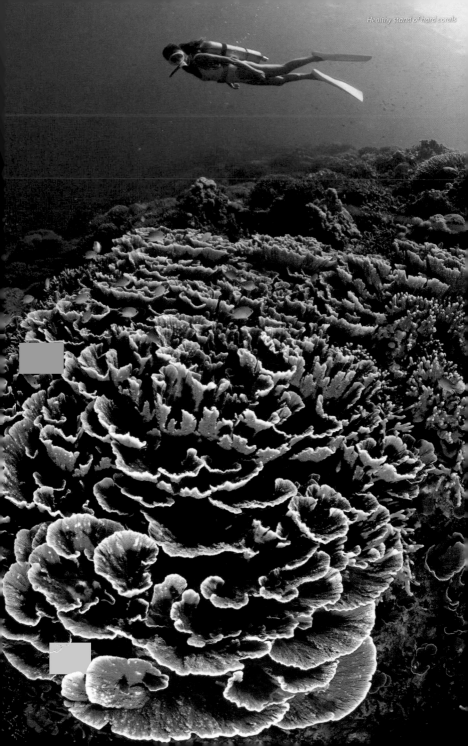

Healthy stand of hard corals

95 MUSHROOM ROCK

Location: *Southeast side of Samal Island*
Depth: *16-115ft (5-35m)*
Access: *Boat*
Range: *Intermediate*

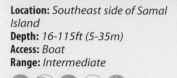

Sticking out of the water, this dive site's namesake rock has been eroded by millennia of unceasing aquatic friction. Watch out for the currents here, as they can be ferocious. For the best conditions, dive this site during the *amihan* (northeast monsoon) season, and at high tide.

The strong currents bring out the pelagics, of course, so you might run into tuna, rainbow runners and jacks, among others. Divers commonly see dolphins in the surrounding area, but seldom encounter them underwater.

The reeftop is well covered with leather corals, table corals and a variety of hard and soft corals. The reef itself has some interesting formations, crevices and bulges that are home to a variety of tropical reef fish. A wall plummets to a sandy bottom at 115ft. Watch your depth on this dive, and remember that currents can pick up fast, so return to your anchor line or shot line with enough air to do a safety stop.

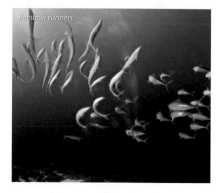
Rainbow runners

96 MARISSA 1, 2 & 3

Location: *S of Samal Island*
Depth: *26-60ft (8-18m)*
Access: *Boat*
Range: *Novice*

Marissa is good training area and not a bad night dive either. Snorkelers may also enjoy this site. Named after the daughter (a keen diver) of the Pearl Farm Resort's owner, the three reefs here share similar features.

The Pearl Farm maintains the reefs as a marine sanctuary, so there is plenty of life bubbling around. The rills, undercuts, small walls and drop-offs interspersed with gentle slopes are home to a variety of corals, including staghorn, elkhorn and table. Moray eels and tube worms vie for space on some parts of the reef, and there is a profusion of sea stars. Seasonal jellies and hydroids can be found here, especially around Easter time. Wear a dive skin to avoid stings.

97 MALIPANO JAPANESE WRECKS

Location: *Off Pearl Farm Resort*
Depth: *60-130ft (18-40m)*
Access: *Boat*
Range: *Advanced*

Though these aren't the most impressive wrecks, they are only about 131ft apart, allowing you to visit two wrecks on the same dive. The lack of currents has prevented much coral from growing on the two hulls of these Japanese ships that went down in WWII.

You'll find nothing particularly outstanding marine life on either – a few sponges and tunicates, a couple of whip corals and the odd shell or two

Decorative patterns of the cowrie

decorate the wreck site – but their proximity to the Pearl Farm Resort has ensured the site is visited frequently. This site is recommended only for those with suitable deep-dive training. Look for a big prop from one ship in the sand.

98	**LINOSUTAN CORAL GARDENS**

Location: *Southeast Talicud Island*
Depth: *16-130ft (5-40m)*
Access: *Boat*
Range: *Novice/intermediate/ advanced*

A good snorkeling site, this 2.5-mile-long stretch of reef offers the closest decent diving to Davao City. Most of the best stuff is above 65ft, but the reef slopes (gently in some places and more steeply in others) down to the sandy bottom at 141ft, with less cover and more sand the deeper you go. Visibility is often good here, usually between 59ft and 88ft. The many species of hard and soft corals make this a colorful and entertaining dive, appreciated by novice and advanced divers alike.

Anthias, shrimp, gobies, damsels, fusiliers, flounder, butterflyfish, sea stars, sponges and tube worms are everywhere. Several species of mollusks navigate the sandy bottom, and you'll find a sizeable colony of ribbon eels, their heads poking out of the sand. It's not uncommon to encounter hawksbill turtles here, and tuna and eagle rays are also frequent visitors.

A great all-round site for photographers, perfect for divers of all skill levels and offering a vast expanse of reef that takes several dives to properly cover, this is one of the best sites Davao has to offer.

GENERAL SANTOS CITY

General Santos City sits on Sarangani Bay and is an education hub for the area as well as a tuna trans-shipment center, thus the nickname 'Tuna City'. It gets daily flights from Manila and divers can grab a cab from the airport for a flat P350 or arrange pickup with the few dive shops here. At night there's an eatery with a foreboding moniker of 'Grab-A-Crab' that has a menu of good Filipino dishes. *Sinugba* is the local specialty – a type of charbroiled tuna (what else?) with its own local sauce.

The reefs won't be crowded here as there are only a few dive shops.

Sarangani Bay is extremely deep, especially at its mouth, so a lot of water flow takes place. Some of the eastern reefs were destroyed by destructive fishing and a crown-of-thorns infestation. But the west bay has many undersea attractions and the reef drop-off is just a short distance from shore and runs for many miles.

General Santos City Dive Sites	GOOD SNORKELING	NOVICE	INTERMEDIATE	ADVANCED
99 MAHARLIKA BEACH RESORT	•	•		
100 TAMPUAN (TINTO WALL)	•			•

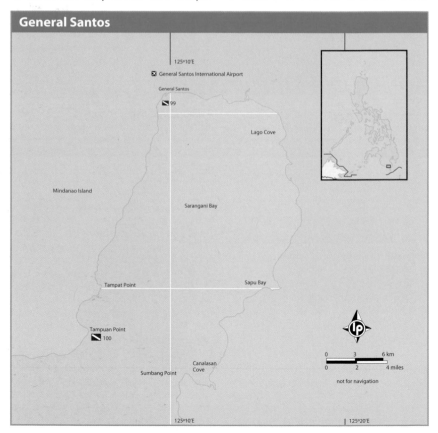

General Santos

Along the reef system a couple of dozen sites, many walk-ins, have been discovered.

Divers can seek such exotic fish as the weedy scorpionfish and an array of nudibranchs, making macro photographers very happy. The area has a number of walk-in sites and even a pier that divers like to visit for the pillar growth.

99 | MAHARLIKA BEACH RESORT

Location: *20mins drive from General Santos*
Depth: *70ft (21m)*
Access: *Shore*
Range: *Novice*

One of the big attractions here is a resident shoal of 500 yellowtail barracuda, but the reef has plenty to offer. It is often used for training and divers and snorkelers enjoy the ease of this walk-in dive. It has healthy coral life with staghorns providing plenty of habitat for smaller fish such as chromis and anthias. The reef is also home to striped sweetlips, rainbow parrotfish, Moorish idols and bannerfish and even some groupers.

Since the reef has so many holes, look for squid egg sacks. If you're lucky, squid can be approached for photos while they are pre-occupied with laying these eggs. There are many pufferfish resting in the hard corals and the lionfish come out to prowl in the late afternoon and can be seen on night dives. The reef has sea snakes prowling as well.

After the dive, divers love to plunge into the natural freshwater spring-fed pool that is found near the beach.

A pufferfish is cleaned by a bluestripe wrasse

100 | TAMPUAN (TINTO WALL)

Location: *31 miles (50km) from General Santos*
Depth: *0-130ft (0-40m)*
Access: *Shore or boat*
Range: *Novice (reeftop), intermediate (wall)*

This reef system is a great spot for divers of all levels and snorkelers of all ages. Healthy corals and plenty of fish mark the upper reef. Most divers drive to one of the popular entry spots. South Point Dive Resort is one site that is good for entry and exploration and Tampat Point at the wall's north end is also popular.

The wall starts a mere 150ft offshore and has a number of dive sites that offer everything from eagle rays and dogtooth tuna to an occasional shark or manta. If you're lucky, dolphins may come in for a look and then swim off.

The real attention grabbers are the beautiful sea fans, big sponges and corals along the wall. With this wall action are many of the usual suspects such as shoaling fusiliers, pyramid butterflyfish, clouds of anthias and red-fang surgeonfish.

For the smaller stuff, look for blue tunicates. Sometimes gobies lay their egg masses on these and guard them, making the gobies easy photo subjects.

A toothy titan triggerfish at a cleaning station

Palawan Dive Sites

Aerial view of the islands around Coron Bay on a misty morning

While most of the Philippines is heavily populated and sectioned out for farming, Palawan is all wide-open spaces. It holds untouched sandy beaches, high limestone cliffs and large tracts of land set aside for cattle grazing. There is still wild jungle here and some rare animals on land and in the sea. The freshwater crocodile is an extremely endangered species, but is found here.

Of the 7000-plus isles in the Philippines, it's said Palawan has 1768 of them. Many are idyllic sandy beaches with coco palms and ruffled jungle. Others are stunning limestone cliffs shield-ing untouched coves and native plant and animal life. It's a pretty place.

Divers have a bonus here: the many islands and bays provided a sheltered and hidden anchorage near Coron that the Japanese used to hide ships during WWII. The ships were discovered and sunk by the US on its quest to retake the Philippines. Now they are coral-laden minireefs full of marine beauty as well as war history.

Divers can fly into El Nido, Puerto Princesa and Busuanga. Busuanga is the airport for those going to the Calamian islands and Coron.

CALAMIAN ISLANDS

One of the most interesting dive areas in Palawan, and at times overlooked due to the fame of the Coron wrecks, is the Calamian group. These islands have a variety of formations that include powder-white sandy beaches, rocky outcrops and towering coconut trees full of fruit bats. They are found along the northern shores of Busuanga Island and out into the north and eastern reef systems of the Mindoro Straits. The outer banks include the famous Apo Reef Natural Park and sites around Tara Islands.

Scenic and diverse, this is a main habitat area for the rare and endangered dugongs, a sea cow that looks some-what like a manatee but has a forked tail like a whale or dolphin. They graze on the sea grasses that grow on the slopes and up into the shallows of many of these islands. Sea turtles, especially green sea turtles, also nest in the islands and munch the grasses.

Calamian Islands Dive Sites	GOOD SNORKELING	NOVICE	INTERMEDIATE	ADVANCED
101 CLUB PARADISE HOUSEREEF	•	•		
102 DIMIPAC ISLAND	•		•	
103 KYOKUZAN MARU	•		•	
104 TARA ISLANDS	•		•	
105 APO REEF	•		•	

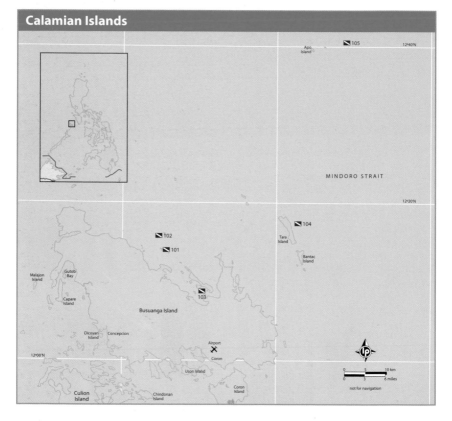

Many of these islands are incredibly photogenic and uninhabited and you can arrange for a day alone or with a special someone on a desert isle, getting a taste of Robinson Crusoe existence (albeit with a well-packed cooler, liquid refreshment and adult beverages). Snorkeling is generally good with minimal currents at most beaches.

Busuanga is served frequently. Get a window seat because on a sunny day, the flight over the islands is like a special tour with stunning tropical colors. One of the most striking aspects about landing here is that there is no city or town below. This is a huge cattle-ranching area and the lack of habitation is a real contrast to most of the Philippines. You then take a 15- to 30-minute jeepney ride on a dirt road that passes over frequent cattle grates and small bridges eventually leading to a dock. Then you board a river ferry that passes healthy mangroves and a fishing village and heads out to some of the area's island-based hotels. It's painless and scenic and a good way to see some of the islands. Most hotels and spas have package deals that can include diving. Instruction, daily dives and special charters can all be arranged.

The island group holds great fish diversity, an array of coral life and also a few war wrecks. The water here is generally quite clear and the presence of the resorts and their group of Coast Guard reserve volunteers has assured dynamiters have not had a presence here. It's a special area in this vast country of islands.

101　CLUB PARADISE HOUSEREEF

Location: *NE of Busuanga*
Depth: *16-56ft (5-17m)*
Access: *Shore or boat*
Range: *Novice to advanced*

One of the friendly hawksbills at Club Paradise Housereef

The site, cleverly named Housereef at Club Paradise, on Dimyaka Island is one of the most interesting in the region, because the reef has been protected as the resort's personal preserve for two decades. And it shows. Turtles graze the sea-grass beds and lay eggs on the beach. Schooling bigeye jacks can be found just offshore in 10ft of water. Look also for big bumphead parrotfish. Giant clams can be found along the reef in a couple of places and it's a great spot for macro oddities such as sleepy sea moths, ornate ghost pipefish, jawfish (at times with eggs), frogfish (large and small), nudibranchs and flatworms.

The corals are varied and a great selection of hard corals and sponges can be seen along the southwest slope. You might also see larger fish such as barracuda and mackerels. Diving here is a walk-in and can be done pretty much any time of day from the Dugong Dive Center kit area right next to the beach. Instruction is done in a pool but also in a natural bowl at about 6ft to 9ft right off the beach. It's a very special kind of classroom.

The main attractions here, however, are the grass munchers. From March to May the area is frequented by dugongs. Sometimes when they see divers they just swim away. But if they are really into feeding they will stay around for a long time. So approach slowly and gradually if you see one and you might have a long dugong encounter. They like the sea grass beds directly in front of the resort. Look for the lawn-mower-like rows in the grass to see where they have been eating. They are usually followed by a cadre of batfish who go after their excrement (ugh!).

Another popular attraction is the constant parade of sea turtles, who enjoy the same grasses. A couple of beautiful green turtles with unblemished shells have become quite accustomed to divers and are like the Housereef pets. They like to have their shells stroked and cleaned and will eat sea grass fed by a diver. They are very good photo subjects and you can watch them dig down to get to the sea-grass roots. This is a lot of work for them so they surface frequently and then come right back down to you.

Many dives can be made at this fascinating reef for both wide-angle and macro photography. Plus, eagle rays and other pelagics do come by here on occasion. The island also has some other sites that have their merits and are no more than 10 minutes by boat.

Dimyaka also has some fascinating birds and land creatures such as monitor lizards and a colony of fruit bats that fly at late dusk. It makes quite a sight if you are just getting into the water for a night dive or just getting out after a mandarinfish dive.

102 DIMIPAC ISLAND

Location: *NW of Dimyaka Island*
Depth: *6-50ft (2-16m)*
Access: *Boat or live-aboard*
Range: *All*

Finger sponges and glassfish

Dugong Watching & Snorkeling

If you want to see one of the most unusual (and endangered) mammals in the sea, full-day excursions (organized through Dugong Dive Center on Dimyaka Island) coupled with a dive or two are available and recommended. Snorkelers will enjoy this tour as well. It is not a guaranteed deal and sometimes if you do see one, the dugong just swims off. But if you get a cooperative lone dugong or a mother and calf, it's an encounter few divers get to experience.

The professionally produced eco-tours begin with a video explaining the dugong's habitat, habits and seasonal sighting, before visiting feeding grounds at Dimyaka, Dimipac, the reserve waters in front of Calauit (where you may also see giraffes on the beach) and coastal northern Busuanga. The trip ends among the islands in a quiet cove as the sun goes down, concluding a full-day excursion that allows you to see a good deal of the area above and below the water.

Dugongs can grow to over 10ft in length and weigh as much as 900lb. A volunteer group from the area, called Dugong Research & Protection, has formed to protect the sea cows. They survey feeding grounds, give lectures to school kids in the surrounding villages and produce educational materials through Club Paradise Resort at Dimyaka Island. Estimates are that there are only 22 or so dugongs in the bay area (not including Tara Islands). Humans are the biggest threat as they catch the dugongs for their meat.

Volunteers from the resorts have joined the Coast Guard auxiliary and can authoritatively do volunteer patrols to protect the dugongs and monitor illegal fishing. As a result, the Calamian group sees little in the way of illegal and destructive fishing. This also leads to a healthy reef and eco-system in the islands.

A dugong munches sea grass
Photo Rolf Winkelhausen

Palm Trees and Giraffes

Unless you're going to South Africa or Kenya, you don't expect to see zebras and giraffes along palm-lined shores. However, there's always a surprise in the Philippines, and in the Calamian Group there's Calauit Island. Back in the days of the Ferdinand Marcos presidency in the mid-1970s, the president was friendly with Kenya and was gifted with a number of animals from the African plains.

Now they thrive on the Calauit Island Game Preserve & Wildlife Sanctuary. Seeing giraffe tracks going down the beach or seeing one towering along with the palms is not unusual but there are always some on an upper open plateau that is about a half-hour safari-truck ride from the boat landing. You can also come from the Coron side.

Rangers will let you hand feed the giraffes. Gazelles, zebras, local Calauit deer, mousedeer and a range of other wildlife can also be seen. There are also some cages near a rest area where you can see local porcupines, freshwater crocodiles (highly endangered) and the reclusive nocturnal bearcat hiding in a tree. Pythons and some other colorful snakes are also found here but are wild, so it's not guaranteed that you'll see any. It's great fun and takes only about a half-day so you can still do some afternoon dives.

A new dive site that doubles as a dugong-watching spot is Dimipac Island, a short ride northwest of Dimakya. The island is uninhabited and has a very nice, sandy beach, which continues down into sea-grass beds where dugongs have been seen grazing. Keep an eye out for clouds of sand, as they really stir things up. But this could also be a pack of goatfish, as they eat in the sand as well.

In front of the beach, the slopes are mainly sea grasses with scattered coral heads and sponges. Look for *Cassiopeia andromeda* (upside-down jellyfish) lying in the sand. Some have leggy crabs underneath that have adopted the jellies just like an anemone hermit crab. Very odd to see a jelly get up and walk away. Take care as these do pack a healthy sting.

There is also a nice path reef system with tube sponges, sea anemones, lots of roaming juvenile-catfish packs and many small things.

103	KYOKUZAN MARU

Location: *E of Busuanga*
Depth: *35-130ft (11-40m)*
Access: *Boat or live-aboard*
Range: *Intermediate*

Whitewall tires on a car in the Kyokuzan hold

Soft coral array

This is one of the best wreck dives in the Coron area as the water here is generally clear with good visibility. The *Kyokuzan Maru* is upright and it sits in a sheltered area with little in the way of currents off Dimalanta Island, so diving here is year-round.

This Japanese freighter was scuttled by its crew when they got word of the attacks in nearby Coron. History reports say the ship was hit by US fire, but there is no evidence of damage to support this. The lifeboat davits have been swung out, so it is believed that after scuttling the ship the crew went to nearby Dimalanta Island.

The wreck sits near a reef, which can be seen from the portside. There are two buoys on the masts of this five-hold freighter – at the fore and aft. It's a bit too deep to get a good look in one dive, so normally (sensibly) two dives are done – each exploring one end of the ship.

Starting aft, the mast and cargo booms are covered in corals, zigzag

Shards of cups in the Kyokuzan

clams and sea anemones. The holds are open and the hold behind the bridge has the remnants (on the port side) of a fancy car that comes complete with whitewalls. The majority of the ship was salvaged after the war – this is true with almost all of the wrecks in the area. But there is still a lot to see. One room under the bridge leading to the engine room holds the remnants of bowls with the Japanese Navy insignia on the shards.

The engine room is also open and you can exit through the stack hole. It is believed the engine was salvaged through this hole. The stack lays on its side leaning to starboard.

For the second dive head up to the massive bow and swim off the front or drop down to the sand to get a perspective of the ship's size – it's 492ft. You can swim under the gun-emplacement area in the bow and down into the holds where you will find more car remnants, truck parts and some odd bales that may be asbestos. Up top around the bridge is where you'll see the marine life. Batfish are ubiquitous, while schooling fusiliers course around the masts. Watch where you put your hands on the deck areas as there are some very big and well-camouflaged stonefish lying around.

The deco stops can be fun, with lots of marine life on the upper booms in the fore as well. Head up the mast to the buoy rope to end the dive.

This area also has a couple of smaller and siltier ships if this isn't enough for your wreck fix. But this ship offers by far the best visibility in the Coron area. Dive shops here do make a trip to the Coron wrecks if divers are interested, but it's an all-day affair. This dive trip can be done in a morning or you can bring along lunch, sleep in and make a relaxing day with a couple of dives and some snorkeling on Dimalanta's nearby reef. There is also a dugong-feeding area not too far away that can be checked out.

The Tara Islands have great soft coral displays

104 | TARA ISLANDS

Location: *South China Sea, W of Mindoro*
Depth: *6-130ft (2-40m)*
Access: *Boat or live-aboard*
Range: *Intermediate*

This is a relatively new area that is being explored for its soft corals and healthy fish populations. It's interesting both undersea and on land, and is home to the indigenous Tagbanua people. They have villages on the major islands and are among the oldest inhabitants of the Philippines. Their rituals and feasts are based on a firm belief in a natural interaction between the world of the living and the world of the dead. They produce unique crafts, such as carved turtles, baskets and mats.

The Tara group is on the way to the Apo Reef and Coron and dives are some-times done here in conjunction with one of those excursions. For extended exploration divers also overnight or go for extended two- or three-day excursions. It's only a 1½-hour boat ride from the resorts around Dimyaka and east Busuanga so three dive days with lunch are the norm. The group has been pioneered just in the last couple of years by local videographer Dirk Fahrenbach. Seven sites have been found so far; five have names, including the **Rock**, **Brown Rocks**, **Cinco**, **Tres Marias** and **Coral Garden**.

Since the islands are far out, the conditions are great – with excellent visibility and currents such as in Apo Reef. Intact soft- and hard-coral gardens combine with sponges in all colors and sizes. The soft corals are best viewed when the currents are moving, which makes them open up, full with color.

The currents also bring in the pelagics. On a typical drift you may encounter gray reef and whitetip sharks, blackbar barracuda shoals, eagle rays, big marble stingrays and large dogtooth tuna. Seasonal manta rays are common especially if the current is strong.

Hairy squat lobster in barrel sponge

For those into the smaller stuff, the reefs also hold pygmy seahorses, a variety of nudibranchs, pink squat lobsters in the folds of the big barrel sponges, anglerfishes and loads of ribbon eels. Bigger fish found here include schooling bumphead parrotfish, bluestripe and yellowtail fusiliers and bigeye jacks, plus many redfang surgeonfishes are found on just about all of the dives.

Tara is great for snorkeling too. The reef plateau is covered with huge table corals and is very intact. The good visibility makes it even possible while snorkeling to see sharks down deep.

And to top it off, there are also three large, sandy sea-grass beds that are great for seeing turtles and are also dugong feeding grounds.

This is new territory and you may want to see it now as it is being explored so that you might be on an expedition that finds yet another new site.

105	APO REEF

Location: *South China Sea, Mindoro Straits (32 miles NE of Busuanga)*
Depth: *7-130ft (2-40m)*
Access: *Boat or Live-aboard*
Range: *Intermediate*

Apo Reef is also a 'natural park' and is one of the premier dive destinations in the country – a must for any Calamian region itinerary. Not to be confused with Apo Island, also a well-kept undersea national park, near Dumaguete, this reef is in open ocean just like its southern counterpart, Tubbataha.

The reef has a dual lagoon system divided by a narrow channel that runs west to east. One small island, also called Apo, has a lighthouse. Like Tubbataha, this is a reef system that offers many dive sites and is good for anywhere from two- to five-day excursions by live-aboard. Area dive shops do make the three-hour journey (it's 32 miles from Busuanga) as a day trip and try to squeeze in three dives when you get there. But that's a long day. Overnight and extended trips allow for a more leisurely pace and lots of exploration. Also like Tubbataha, there's little protection from the elements. January to June is considered the season for this area although some nearby dive shops may attempt it if conditions look to be calm in the off season.

Shark Ridge, **Binangaan Drop-off** and **North Wall** are some of the famous sites. At these, and others, a diver can expect to see big fish such as dogtooth tuna, whitetip, blacktip and gray reef sharks, wahoo, Spanish mackerel, Napoleon wrasse and bumphead parrotfish. Flowing currents can bring in mantas, barracuda schools, bigeye jacks and even tiger sharks. Over 400 species of fish and 500 corals have been identified here.

The reef has a past history of dynamite fishing although it has been well protected in recent years. For this protection there is a P1300 (US$28) park fee to keep the rangers in food and gas. Some of the upper reef show these past ravages but, on the whole, it's a very healthy reef system and the walls are spectacular. Big gorgonian fans, black coral trees, barrel sponges and soft, very nice, cotton-candy coral gorgonians can be found on this wall. The coral formation at the reef plateau is also stunning.

Hunter's Rock, about 13 miles away, used to be a popular dive site for pelagics as well. But it is not patrolled or protected like Apo and blast fishing has taken its toll. Also, currents can be wicked so it's not for the novice. Most dive operators recommend the experience will be best by staying at Apo.

Barrel sponges, sea fans and sponges make Apo colorful

CORON BAY

If you fly into Busuanga and don't head to the Calamians, the road going the other way through cattle country is the one to Coron. This town has become the wreck-diving capital of the Philippines.

The area near town is known for a rare bird, the balinsasayaw, found in the numerous caves there. You can watch harvesters gather their nests for bird's-nest soup. The town has a nice selection of locally designed T-shirts and traditional handicrafts at Corong Galeri Lokals. Like El Nido, this bay area also

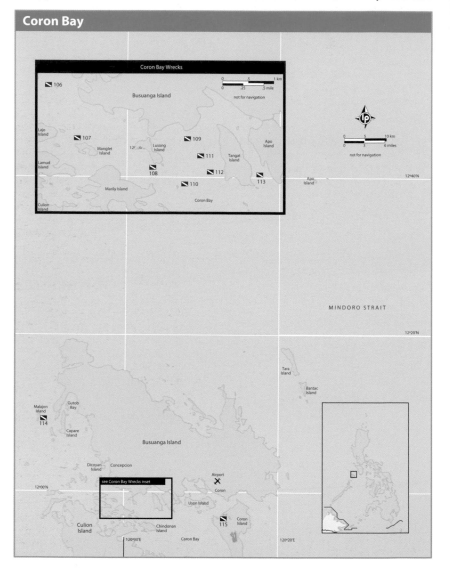

Coron Bay

has impressive limestone cliffs, most notably those surrounding Coron Island. There are sheltered, beautiful saltwater lakes that can be explored by kayak and with a snorkel.

Coron Bay is a large sheltered body of water that was a perfect anchorage for Japan's ships during WWII. Thanks to that shelter, diving is possible all year here; the drawback of the shelter is that there isn't much water movement so visibility can vary greatly. On a good day visibility might get up to 82ft, but be prepared for less. Visibility is best between January and May and can be consistently very low from June through November.

There are a number of dive centers to choose from here. Tech diving is quite popular – Technical Diving International/Scuba Diving International (TDI/SDI) and Professional Association of Diving Instructors (PADI) courses are offered. The relative lack of currents on most wrecks and the depths of some of the wrecks lends itself perfectly to both the training and practice of technical diving. All of the ships have mooring buoys and lines going down to the wrecks.

There are also a couple of reefs around for those who get tired of wrecks. The **Sangat Housereef** is a favorite night dive and is said to have big and active jawfish, while the suspiciously named **Dynamite Reef** is good for macro folks.

| 106 | OKIKAWA MARU |

Location: *SW of Concepcion*
Depth: *33-85ft (10-26m)*
Access: *Boat*
Range: *Intermediate*

The *Okikawa Maru* (sometimes called the Concepcion Wreck) is a huge ship, over 550ft in length. It was a civilian oil tanker pressed into military service. Sunk during the 1944 air raid, its most remarkable feature is the bizarrely bent and disfigured bow. This may be in part due to the huge ship sinking nose first and crashing to the sea floor. Divers can enter one of the upper deck cargo areas and swim through the bow wreckage. All of the ships were salvaged and the highlight of a dive here for the experienced wreckie is penetration through the propeller shaft.

The deck lies between 35ft at the bridge and about 50ft towards the bow. It is not particularly deep – at 85ft to the sand – but currents can be strong as it sits in a channel. Divers can hide from the currents by staying on the ship's lee. Visibility is often less than 30ft.

However, the currents feed the corals and that makes this one of the best ships for wreck coral and sponge growth, which includes a profusion of healthy cabbage corals, a variety of sponges, and hard and sort corals of all sorts. Also look on the deck for Nembrotha and *Flabellina sp* nudibranchs and colorful flatworms.

A shoal of barracuda often circles divers, and you're likely to encounter sweetlips, groupers, batfish, lionfish, surgeons and feeding mackerel. Large jellyfish often drift by in the currents.

Coron Bay Dive Sites	GOOD SNORKELING	NOVICE	INTERMEDIATE	ADVANCED
106 OKIKAWA MARU		•	•	
107 AKITSUSHIMA (SEAPLANE TENDER SHIP)	•		•	
108 LUSONG GUNBOAT	•		•	
109 OLYMPIA MARU	•		•	
110 IRAKO	•		•	
111 KOGYU MARU	•		•	
112 TANGAT WRECK	•		•	
113 TANGAT GUNBOAT	•	•		
114 BLACK ISLAND WRECK			•	
115 1BARRACUDA LAKE (CAYANGAN LAKE)				

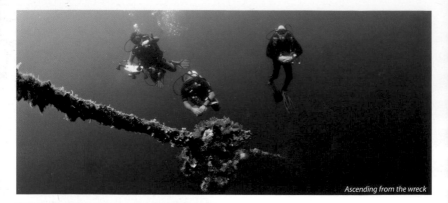

Ascending from the wreck

107 AKITSUSHIMA (SEA PLANE TENDER SHIP)

Location: *2 miles (3.2km) SE of Pompion Caye*
Depth: *60-125ft (18-36m)*
Access: *Boat*
Range: *Advanced*

Although this is one of the deepest wrecks in the area, you'll see plenty without descending beyond 80ft. The ship was a sea-plane tender ship – the only actual warship sunk in the attack. You can see the anti-aircraft guns amidships and forward. There is no sign of any planes, but the crane that was used to lower the planes into the sea sits off the port aft and stretches out into the sandy sea floor at 118ft.

The wreck is penetrable through a huge crack midship. Divers can enter here with a guide and see lots of twisted metal and clouds of glassfish. Very photogenic. And check out the engine room, which escaped the salvagers and still has its engine.

At around 500ft long, *Akitsushima* is one of the largest wrecks in the area and is another popular technical dive. It's known particularly for a huge school of batfish that hang around. Tuna, barracuda and yellowfins frequently patrol

the wreck. Lionfish, groupers, sweetlips and snappers hide inside it. There are also some nice growths of black coral.

108 LUSONG GUNBOAT

Location: *S of Lusong Island*
Depth: *0-33ft (0-10m)*
Access: *Boat*
Range: *Novice*

Both the wreck and the reef adjacent to this small gunboat are an easy dive and excellent snorkeling site. At low tide, the jagged stern of the 140ft ship actually breaks the surface. This is a perfect introductory wreck dive and, because of its shallow depth, is also a good choice for a second or third dive of the day. It's also great for snorkelers who want to see a war wreck.

Lots of soft corals and sponges dot the site, while many pufferfish, angelfish, batfish and butterflyfish flit about. Moray eels like the cracks and holes. Not much of the wreck remains, but this is a good site for photographers, as there is usually little current and lots of light illuminating the variety of subjects. Look especially for cuttlefish, who seem to like to go through mating rituals in the area.

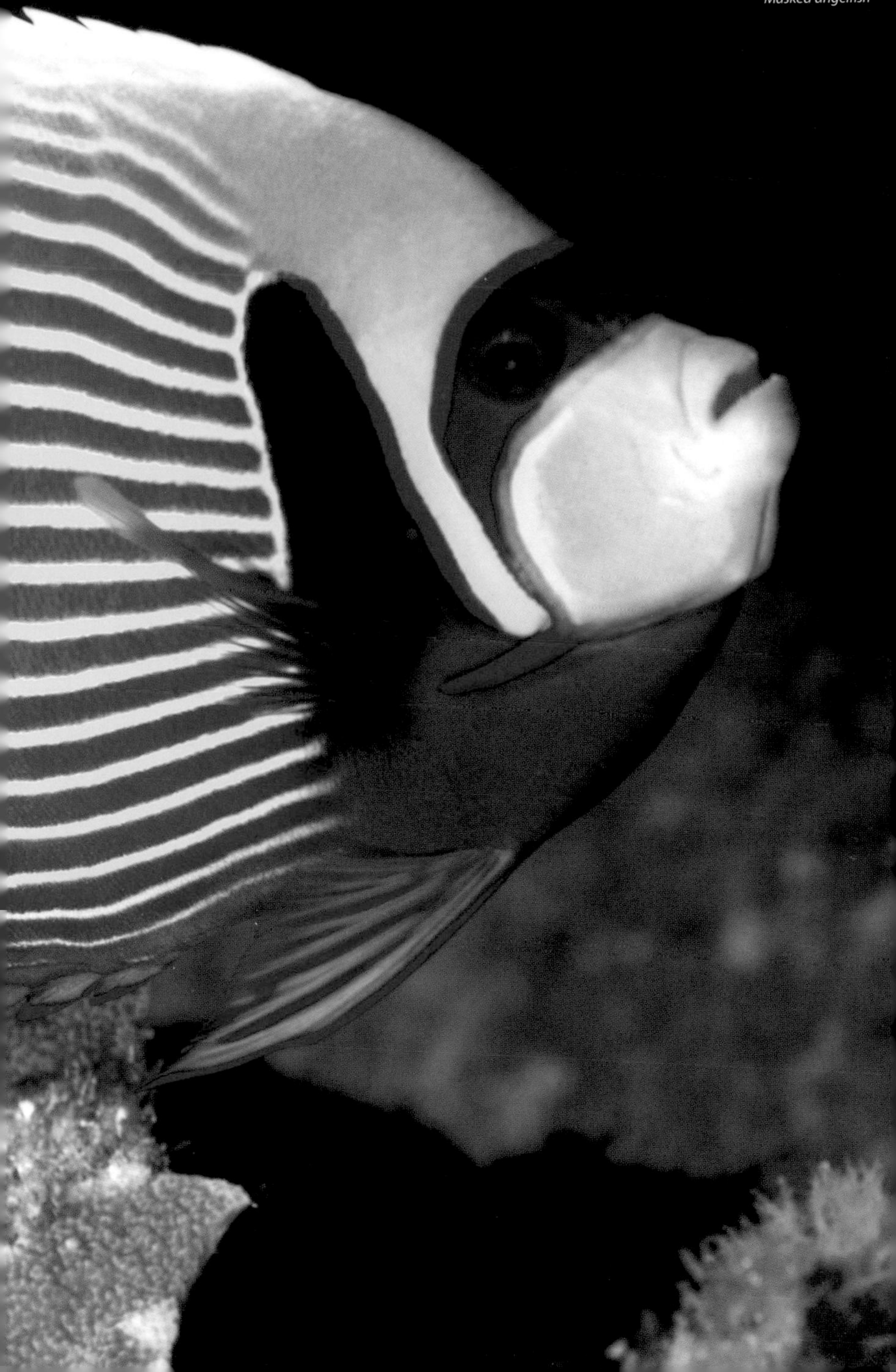
Masked angelfish

One stripe clownfish in purple anemone

for nudibranchs and headshield slugs on the ship.

For some good lionfish shots, swim to the bow where you will see many of the stealthy stalkers. Watch where you put your hands as large scorpionfish hide in the vessel's nooks and crannies.

Remember, the ship is on its side and it's easy to get disoriented, so follow a guide. Sometimes the current can also be a factor. The buoy line is attached to the large rudder.

This is also a popular training site for advanced and wreck diving classes.

110 IRAKO

Location: *Between Tangat and Lusong Islands*
Depth: *100-138ft (30-42m)*
Access: *Boat*
Range: *Advanced*

109 OLYMPIA MARU

Location: *Between Lusong and Tangat Islands*
Depth: *40-82ft (12-25m)*
Access: *Boat*
Range: *Intermediate*

Lying on its starboard side, this wreck features black coral, finger sponges and a variety of soft and hard corals encrusted along its 400ft-long hull. There is a damage hole on the port side below the bridge that appears to be what did the ship in. Divers can inspect all of the open cargo holds and even enter the bridge through the hold nearest to it. You can also enter and exit through the damage hole. One particularly impressive feature is the huge engine boiler that still remains on the ship.

You'll find lots of anemones and clownfish, as well as resident batfish, a couple of large groupers and many smaller ones, goatfish and fusiliers. Look

Wreck penetration should be done with care

A stairway at a ship's bridge

This wreck is deeper than most in the bay and experiences strong currents at times, so it's for the more-advanced diver. It is a good penetrable wreck, but because of its depth (it sits upright with its deck sloping from 80ft at the bow to 100ft at deck level) and size (about 500ft long), safe penetration requires specialized training and an experienced guide.

The *Irako* was a refrigeration ship and you can see the cooling pipes in the holds. There is heavy siltation on the wreck, but those with excellent buoyancy and wreck training can penetrate to see the pots and pans in the galley and the inner bomb damage. It is a tricky, but interesting, penetration.

Some big groupers call this home now, and you may also see shoals of barracuda and yellowfin tuna circling the site in the currents. Look for batfish, snappers, some wrasses and lots of lionfish and scorpionfish around the wreck. The hull and deck are quite well covered in a variety of soft corals and sponges. Again, the current can get quite strong here, so plan your dive well.

111 KOGYU MARU

Location: *S of Olympia Maru*
Depth: *60-112ft (18-34m)*
Access: *Boat*
Range: *Advanced*

According to war records, this supply ship had very poor timing. It came in from Subic Bay the day before the attack and so got there just in time to be bombed. *Kogyu Maru* is a deep wreck, nearly 500ft long, lying on its starboard side. It has some pretty hard and soft corals on its exposed port hull.

The holds are open and the jumbled contents include a bulldozer and a cargo of cement bags, jumbled wire and other junk in the silt. The four large cargo booms have lots of marine growth and are good to explore and swim through.

Like many of the other ships, lionfish thrive here, and you'll likely see a shoal of barracuda and a reasonable assortment of tropical reef fish.

The wreck is deep, and bottom time is limited, so it's not for all scuba divers. But technical divers enjoy this dive, and it is a good technical training dive.

112 | TANGAT WRECK

Location: *Off SW point of Tangat Island*
Depth: *60-100ft (18-30m)*
Access: *Boat*
Range: *Intermediate*

Encrusting marine life on the hull

Another good site for underwater photographers is the *Tangat* wreck. It is also known as Sangat wreck as it's just a 10-minute boat ride from the Sangat Resort. The ship is about 400ft long and is covered with lots of soft corals, purple and blue sponges and some hard corals. It's a very good wreck for marine life and the masts and cargo booms are covered in corals and encrusting marine organisms.

The wreck lies more or less upright. The cargo holds, which are easily accessible, are home to angelfish, snappers and batfish, among others. Those wanting to penetrate can enter the aft hold and swim through to the next. You can then head through the boiler room and exit midships near the bridge. This is a good training wreck but is also popular with experienced wreck divers.

Several large, friendly pufferfish make for accommodating photo subjects. Cockatoo waspfish can be seen and cuttlefish also like the ship. Look for clouds of photogenic glassfish in the black coral trees along with lionfish in their midst. The currents are usually quite light, but can occasionally pick up.

113 | TANGAT GUNBOAT

Location: *E of Tangat Island*
Depth: *7-60ft (2-18m)*
Access: *Boat*
Range: *Novice*

Tangat Gunboat is another great snorkeling site and an easy diving site. The 110ft-long vessel lies just off the rocky east coast of Tangat Island, with its bow about 6ft from the surface. It's easy to find, as you can see the wreck clearly from the surface. It lies right next to a reef as well.

Not a lot of coral grows on the wreck, and visibility is not usually very good,

Look for cardinalfish on the wrecks

but there are some interesting invertebrates, and some lettuce sponges and a few small reef fish – including harlequin ghost pipefish and striped pipefish – call it home. Look for crabs and shrimp. On a night dive, the bright shrimp eyes flash out when the dive light hits them.

This is a popular site with kayakers as well.

114 BLACK ISLAND WRECK

Location: *NW of Busuanga, E of Malajon Island*
Depth: *55-115ft (17-35m)*
Access: *Boat*
Range: *Advanced*

Not far offshore from Malajon Island, Black Island Wreck sits upright on the sloping sandy bottom. It is sometimes called the *Nanshin Maru* although there seems to be some controversy about the exact name of the ship. It's on a slope with the stern at 65ft and the bow at 100ft. This is the northernmost of the Coron wrecks and it takes about an hour to get to the site.

Little is known about this wreck. Unlike most of the region's wrecks, it wasn't sunk during the September 1944 air raid and may not even be of Japanese construction. Like Palau's Helmet Wreck, it may be a spoil of war from another nation, converted for war use. It is a tanker designed to carry specific fuels, which were placed in separate tanks and used to restock the fuel supply of the land depots. The tankers were part of the Japanese Imperial Army.

It's not within the sheltered confines of Coron Bay, but many make the trip as it's still a favorite for wreck-diving training. It does have generally strong currents, which brings fish life. And the visibility is generally good, making it popular with photographers.

Named for the black rocks of adjacent Malajon Island, the wreck is home to lots of sweepers, shoals of snappers, fusiliers, several different species of angelfish including the beautiful six-banded angels and the emperor. The wreck also has groupers and (surprise) scorpionfish and lionfish. Sponge life is also nice.

115	BARRACUDA LAKE (CAYANGAN LAKE)

Location: *Coron Island*
Depth: *0-130ft (0-40m)*
Access: *Boat and a hike*
Range: *Intermediate to advanced*

One of the most unusual diving and snorkeling sites in the Philippines, Barracuda Lake is an inland body of water. It's a little climb up through the limestone forest and down. The view looking down into the lake is worth the climb.

The lake is fed by a freshwater hot spring, seawater intruding from deep subterranean cracks and more freshwater from rain and other springs. As a result, at different depths you'll experience extremes in temperature (thermoclines) and salinity (haloclines). Temperatures can range from 85°F to 105°F (30°C to 40°C) and can change several degrees over just a few centimeters' depth. You can see the shimmering layers of different temperatures and salinity as you descend.

There's not a lot of marine life, but a curious mix of shrimp, crustaceans, rabbitfish and a few snappers, among others, call this home. There is a resident barracuda (thus the name) and many cardinalfish and small catfish schools.

The water is really clear so you can see up and down the limestone cliffs that border this rarity. As it is a lake, there is no current.

Getting to the site requires a climb with your gear on. With snorkel gear it's not bad; with dive gear, one should be a bit fit or tip the guide well if he brings your tank for you (shame). You go up from the beach through a gap in the cliff and then along the winding track up and over sharp limestone. Wear strong-soled booties or you may slip or cut your feet.

Take a camera! The scenery is magnificent; the lake is turquoise blue and, if you're lucky, the lake's star attraction, a 1.5m barracuda, may make an appearance, look for a handout and even escort you around the lake.

EL NIDO

This may be one of the most scenic areas in the country, with towering limestone cliffs a la Palau's Rock Islands or Phi Phi, Thailand. Blessed with extraordinary natural scenery, El Nido is one of the country's main natural attractions and has been hosting tourism for a couple of decades.

The El Nido Marine Reserve Park is a large and diverse ecosystem of rainforest, mangroves, fine-sand beaches, coral reefs and limestone cliffs. It is now one of the country's premier tourist destinations.

It used to be quite an overland trip to get here from Puerto Princesa. But now there are daily direct flights from Manila (sometimes twice daily), plus hops from Busuanga and Puerto Princesa as well. There aren't many places to stay, which is nice in a way as it makes the reefs pretty uncrowded. Some resorts are also on private islands, adding to the charm.

Dive centers and hotels are doing their best to keep dynamiters away but the area's reefs do have blast damages in places. Overall, there are about 20-plus dive sites in the El Nido area.

El Nido Dive Sites	GOOD SNORKELING	NOVICE	INTERMEDIATE	ADVANCED
116 DILUMACAD		•	•	
117 TRES MARIAS		•		•
118 MINILOC ISLAND		•		•

116   DILUMACAD

Location: *Northern tip of Dilumacad Island*
Depth: *33-82ft (10-25m)*
Access: *Boat*
Range: *Intermediate*

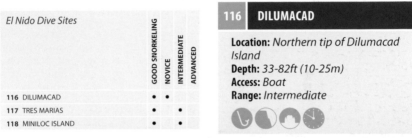

El Nido

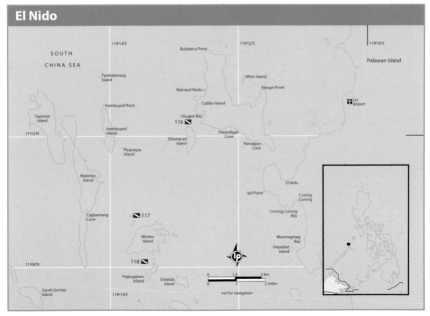

A feather star on a sea fan

This site has one particular feature that makes it very popular: a cave big enough for a pair of divers that starts at about 40ft. It's more of a tunnel actually that opens out at 70ft after narrowing down a bit. The sandy bottom holds shells and crabs. After exiting, you can rummage around moving slowly shallower among the large rocks. Look for big fish such as bull jacks and Spanish mackerel.

This dive is close to most of the hotels and dive centers and can be dived year-round, except when the wind comes down from the north.

117 TRES MARIAS

Location: *Tabago Island, NW of Miniloc Island*
Depth: *16-92ft (5-28m)*
Access: *Boat*
Range: *Intermediate*

This site is good for both divers and snorkelers. Starting in about 15ft of water, it presents big boulders and rocks to play in and explore. Expect to see lots of fish – both adult and juvenile – hiding among the cracks and crevices. And lobsters really like this habitat – they are sometimes found in groups with their antennae waving curiously as you approach. Fish lovers will want to keep an eye and lens out for the beautiful blue-ring angels here: there is an endemic blue-ring pomachanthid with an extra stripe that is said to be found only here and at the nearby Inambuyod Boulders dive site.

118 MINILOC ISLAND

Location: *SW Bacuit Bay*
Depth: *42-70ft (13-21m)*
Access: *Boat*
Range: *Novice*

This popular island dive can be done all year. It has two sites: South Miniloc and Twin Rocks. They do start a bit deep but snorkelers go here as well as divers, and instructors use the area for some training too.

South Miniloc is known for its nice lettuce corals, sponges and blue ribbon eels. Sometimes they are here in good numbers and seem to form a colony. This is a good site for cuttlefish, who mate and lay eggs here. Angels, parrotfish, jacks and barracuda are all part of the reef scene.

Twin Rocks is north of Miniloc and has a somewhat different terrain, with big table corals, sponges, small tunicate colonies resembling bouquets, hard corals and colorful sea whips. Blue-spotted rays enjoy the sandy bottom.

Chromis in table coral

PORT BARTON

This sleepy fishing-village town on Palawan's western coast is a real get-away-from-it-all kind of dive destination. The sunsets are great. It has very reasonably priced beach bungalows and small hotels, powder-sand beaches and diving on reefs and islands off the village and in Pagdanan Bay. Unless you call drinking beer in the moonlight 'nightlife', you'll find the place pretty quiet. It has some no-power hours but divers with camera/strobe batteries to charge should be OK as power hours are normally 4pm until midnight or so, and hotels have generators (although they aren't always in use). So plug your stuff in right after your dive day and carry a few extra batteries.

It's a bit of a drive to get there: a bone-jarring public jeepney is really cheap but takes as long as six hours from Puerto Princesa. Private van or private jeepneys are under US$100 and more like a four-hour jaunt.

Once there you find sites for dive training, sites for the more experienced and sites that snorkelers will really enjoy. The low prices are making this a backpackers' favorite haunt. March to August is best for diving but most sites are good all year.

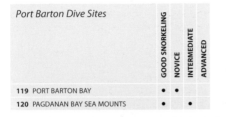

Port Barton Dive Sites	GOOD SNORKELING	NOVICE	INTERMEDIATE	ADVANCED
119 PORT BARTON BAY	•	•		
120 PAGDANAN BAY SEA MOUNTS	•		•	

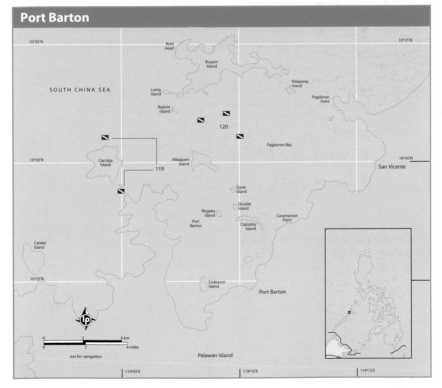

Port Barton

Diver and sea turtle

119 | PORT BARTON BAY

Location: *40mins or less from Port Barton*
Depth: *0-108ft (0-33m)*
Access: *Boat*
Range: *Intermediate*

Three dives located just outside the bay include Shark Point off northern Cacnipa Island, Middle Rock on the other side of the island and Black Coral across the bay off Cone Island.

Shark Point is actually a rock that starts at the surface and falls down to 108ft. The main attractions are the many hard and soft corals, as well as the holes and small caves that hold critters like painted lobsters. There is also a cavern, where whitetip sharks sometimes rest.

Currents are normally minimal. Thus, divers can circumnavigate Shark Point in one dive.

Middle Rock is also a rock-dive site that starts at the surface and falls down to about 100ft. It is home to a school of bumphead parrotfish, and lots of anthias float colorfully over the rocks and corals. At both Shark Point and Middle Rock, seas can be a bit bumpy if swells from the South China Sea are in play, but there's usually lee shelter to suit up and jump in. Again, Middle Rock is normally not too bad for currents.

Across the bay, **Black Coral** starts in 16ft of water and drops down a bit past 80ft. This is a coral reef with a nice cavern that holds a cleaning station with shrimp, a big school of glassfish and other wrasse-managed cleaning stations. The black corals that give the dive its name are found as large 'trees' at about 60ft past the cavern along the wall.

120 PAGDANAN BAY SEAMOUNTS

Location: *W of Port Barton*
Depth: *10-130ft (3-40+m)*
Access: *Boat*
Range: *Intermediate to advanced*

Three more dive sites for the somewhat more experienced are found in the open sea of Pagdanan Bay. **Royalist Shoal** starts in 40ft of water and has steep walls that have some of the area's nicest soft corals. Follow your guide down and drop over the side checking out the habitat of soldierfish, tangs, angels and lots more. It's a very fishy place.

Nearby, **Ten Fathoms** is another seamount, which starts in 60ft depths and also offers the chance to see fish, although many of these are pelagics or water-column dwellers such as hammerhead sharks and tuna. Leopard and nurse sharks are also reported swimming freely or resting in a niche on the reef. The reef has a good selection of hard, soft and even pillar corals as well as lots of smaller reef fish. Currents and depth are a factor here so watch your guide and your air.

The next site, **Wilson Head**, can be more diver friendly but also has its deep side. Snorkelers like the reeftop as it starts in just 10ft of water. Look for some healthy old-growth corals here including some nice brain corals. This is a good spot for crustaceans, including painted lobsters and a variety of crabs.

Sea fans, red sea whips, a variety of anemones and clownfish and many other invertebrates and fish make this a good photo site worth a couple of dives.

Masked rabbitfish

PUERTO PRINCESA & ENVIRONS

While this city is best known to traveling divers as the place you get on a ship to go to the Sulu Sea, it is a popular resort area for Filipinos. A lot of training goes on here and some muck and macro dive sites close to town provide places for photographers to seek images of colorful nudibranchs and a mimic octopus or two. These can be seen as close as the outer shores of Puerto Princesa Bay.

The friendly, laid-back city sprawls around the bays and into the hills. It's the hub of the area, with several daily flights from Manila plus ferries and a crossroads of land routes. The city is easy to get around and has an active market. Many divers spend an extra day or two here to wind down after a Sulu Sea trip. Others like the resort environment for diving-course work. Island-hopping trips can be arranged if you just want to lounge in Honda Bay's islands.

This area, like Donsol, also has fireflies along the river. It's a cool lightshow and you can combine it with a sunset cruise on the Iwahig River. The underground river tour is also highly touted and very popular. At night, check the grilled tuna panga, ginger crabs or some steamed *lapu lapu* (grouper). Seafood is a great deal here.

The sites below are found a bit north of the city in Honda Bay. This bay is affected by the seasonal prevailing winds but is very easy on the eyes, with numerous islands and shallow reefs. Many of them, however, have been affected by blast fishing.

The Dos Palmas Resort and Spa has established its own marine research center in an effort to protect the reefs in and around its Arreceffi Island base. There are also a couple of dive sites there.

Puerto Princesa & Environs Dive Sites	GOOD SNORKELING	NOVICE	INTERMEDIATE	ADVANCED
121 VERANO ROCKS (TWIN ROCKS)	•	•		
122 EAST PANDAN REEF	•		•	
123 HELEN'S GARDEN/HENRY'S REEF	•		•	

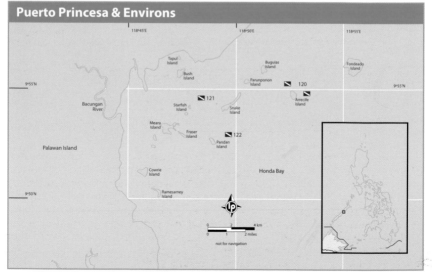

Yellow-eye pufferfish

121 VERANO ROCKS (TWIN ROCKS)

Location: *NE of Starfish Island*
Depth: *33-60ft (10-18m)*
Access: *Boat*
Range: *Novice*

This site is popular because it is generally protected from the prevailing *amihan* and *hagabat* – so it can be dived in all but the worst conditions. There are two coral-reef systems here, northeast of Starfish Island, that slope down to about 60ft. Look for the maze of black coral that forms a bridge between the two reefs. Lots of small fish and lionfish like to hide in the branches. Arrow crabs may make a nice image here.

Snorkelers like the upper reef, where the anemones have a variety of clownfish. There are also some schooling yellowtail snappers, fusiliers and hiding puffers.

122 EAST PANDAN REEF

Location: *E of Pandan Reef*
Depth: *33-56ft (10-17m)*
Access: *Shore or boat*
Range: *Novice*

South of Starfish Island is the larger Pandan Island, which has a fringing reef featuring a steep slope (leading to a sandy sea floor) full of smaller fish, corals and sandy patches. Blue-spotted rays, nesting triggerfish and parrotfish can be found here. Also, look in the sand for gobies and around the coral heads for blennies.

123 HELEN'S GARDEN/HENRY'S REEF

Location: *NW of Dos Palmas Resort, Arreceffi Island*
Depth: *16-60ft (5-18m)*
Access: *Shore or boat*
Range: *Novice*

Helen's Garden is one of the sites of the Dos Palmas Resort and it normally has clear water and lots to see. This reef area is watched by the hotel staff and folks at its research center, so it's healthy and less affected by illegal fishing practices than other area reefs. It's also an easy and favorite night dive.

Table corals, leather soft corals and even some black corals make this small, circular reef home. Giant clams have been placed here and divers can feed fish near the big tridacnas. Divers and snorkelers alike can enjoy the blast of flash and color as the fish vie for bits of food. Keep an eye out for juvenile black-tip sharks, as the area is also a nursery for them.

Henry's Reef is a bit south and is bigger and longer than Helen's. It runs down the entire east coast of Arreceffi Island, and even has a mini-wall running from 15ft to 35ft. Look into the small caves and many crevices on the wall for lionfish, cardinalfish and numerous nudibranchs. Sweetlips line up at cleaning stations here and soldierfish like the crevices.

This is also a good snorkeling site, and the wall is a nice spot for a free dive. Photographers like the site and night divers say they see lots of critters crawling around. It is best dived when the *amihan* isn't blowing, due to its exposure.

Giant clams have been placed at Helen's Garden

The Sulu Sea Dive Sites

The Sulu Sea (loudly and proudly) boasts a Unesco World Heritage site and 'natural park' proclaimed Tubbataha National Marine Park in 1988. The Philippine government seems to be doing its best to protect this special series of sunken atolls and seamounts from poachers and dynamite fishing. That's good news for divers, as this is truly one of the finest dive destinations in the Indo-Pacific.

Diving here is seasonal, running from March into June when the seas are normally flat and calm. There is no real protection for ships out here as the few islands are little more than sand bars and coconut-palm sand spits. Live-aboard ships are normally pretty full so it pays to book in advance, although there can be some good deals arising from last minute cancellations. The ships normally leave from Puerto Princesa in Palawan, on trips averaging five days.

Each visitor to the park (also known locally as the Tubbataha Reefs Natural Park) pays a conservation fee of P3000 (roughly US$60) and this is usually included in the live-aboard fee. This revenue is used to manage, maintain and improve the park. It finances law enforcement and education campaigns, facilities and boat maintenance and training for rangers. Divers get a plastic badge to clip onto their buoyancy control device to show support and fee payment. These rangers, who come from various public and private conservation and enforcement organizations, are there year-round.

This is an important site biologically. The area is described by marine scientists as a spawning and grow-out sanctuary for corals and fishes. This spawn may be carried by oceanic currents to replenish coastal reefs, not only in Palawan and the Visayan islands, but as far south as Malaysia and Indonesia.

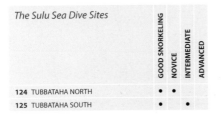

The Sulu Sea Dive Sites	GOOD SNORKELING	NOVICE	INTERMEDIATE	ADVANCED
124 TUBBATAHA NORTH		•	•	
125 TUBBATAHA SOUTH		•		•

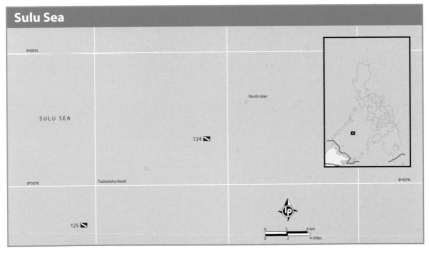

Lionfish at cleaning station at South Airport

For divers, the dives here are the ultimate wall experience with lots of healthy corals, including big gorgonian fans and colorful soft corals. The shallow reeftop is mostly healthy; there are some dynamited areas, but generally it is a huge bed of staghorn and other Acroporas with tons of fish. Anthias and pyramid butterflyfish abound along the upper reef and drop-off.

This is one of the best places in the Philippines for a chance at seeing Mr Big Manta rays, and hammerhead sharks, gray reef sharks, tiger sharks, yellowfin tuna and even oceanic whitetip sharks have all been reported. Dogtooth tuna, large jacks and wahoo are also seen, while big marble rays and lots of sea turtles are reef residents.

The Jesse Beazely seamount and Basterra used to be part of a trip here, but they are hard for the rangers to patrol and poachers and dynamiters have made these reefs less desirable. So a week of diving is normally just done at North and South Tubbataha. (The official website for Tubbataha is www.tubbataha reef.org.)

| 124 | **TUBBATAHA NORTH** |

Location: *110 miles SE of Puerto Princesa*
Depth: *0-130ft (0-40m)*
Access: *Live-aboard*
Range: *Intermediate*

A week of live-aboard diving may start at Shark Airport and run from North Tubbataha to the south, diving at different sites along the way depending on what the wind is doing. There's not a lot of relief here so your ship will normally anchor in the lee.

Shark Airport has a series of sandy channels leading out to a wall and is a great spot to see sea turtles, eagle rays and lots of various jack species. Whitetip reef sharks rest in many of the sand valleys here like planes on a tarmac, thus the name. The wall has schooling bannerfish, bigeye jacks and unicornfish. Look for some great undercuts along the wall areas with soft corals and sea fans. Huge barrel sponges can be found from about 40ft into the depths. Look closely at these giant sponges for the tiny hairy squat lobster (Laura seagoing) that lives in their deep folds. They also serve as shelter and cleaning stations for various fish.

South Shark Airport has a beautiful series of sandy channels as well. It also has a manta-ray cleaning station where lucky divers might see some action. The station itself is very photogenic with healthy corals, clouds of anthias and tiny baitfish and a lot of hovering and lurking lionfish.

The **Washing Machine** is a current drift starting almost under the mooring you will find in this area. The term refers to the surface chop seen here, not the underwater conditions. Lots of Napoleon wrasse can be seen along the wall and in the upper coral gardens, together with masses of schooling tangs. Also keep an eye out for big jack schools: a school moving above the healthy reef makes a pretty photo. This site has good sea-turtle action and also some ubiquitous resting whitetips. At one point in the dive along the upper inner reef there is old dynamite damage at 25ft to 40ft in what were once nice gardens. Nearby are some huge old coral heads rising more than 20ft from the reef, and there is a point at 50ft to 60ft with deep cuts and lots of fish life.

On all of these sites, look for shallow schooling bigeye jacks – often you will see giant trevally harassing the school. Blue-stripe jacks, cruising marble rays, shark life (including gray reef sharks in blue water), Napoleon wrasses and lots of chromis and anthias are found up top. The sandy patches hold the homes of gobies and bulldozer shrimp and garden eels, while the corals and cracks are home to lots of starfish and some nice nudibranchs. After the dives, watch the sea birds moving in and out of Bird Islet.

Another popular site is an old wreck –

Tubbataha Bird Islet

The Tubbataha Bird Islet is an uninhabited sandy isle in the north of Tubbataha North where sea turtles lay their eggs and sea birds breed. Of the more-than-7000 islands in the Philippines, these 12,000 sq meters comprise the only bird sanctuary off limits and highly restricted to humans. The birds living here include the black noddy, brown noddy, white egret, red-footed booby, brown booby, crested tern, sooty tern, lesser frigate bird, greater frigate bird, Christmas Island frigate bird, plover and whimbrel.

dubbed the **Malayan Wreck** – in view of the ranger station. It is pretty well broken up and has become a large cleaning station, attracting a wide variety of fish – both resident and passing through for a clean. If diving in the evening, watch quietly and you'll see two kinds of sweetlips, groupers and even a huge, but shy, resident Napoleon wrasse all lined up for a cleaning, plus myriad smaller fishes.

Shallow and a bit jagged in places, the wreck has a couple of swim-throughs but mostly it is just a great fish refuge. Those that love blennies will find the nearby reeftop a great stop for the red-speckled variety. Macrophotographers will want to stake out their holes for a shot of these comical and pretty fish.

Remnants of the Malayan Wreck

Hanging soft-coral garden

There is also a large, resident crocodile-fish that lurks here.

This is not considered to be an entire dive on its own, so divers usually also head out to the nearby wall where there are normally turtles, especially at lower tides, bigeye jacks and lots of red fang triggerfish. And we do mean lots!

This is also the site of a blue-water dive at sunrise to seek a peek at schooling scalloped hammerhead sharks. Divers get up when it's still dark and try to be in the water at first light. This is normally done only if there is only slight or minimal current to ensure people don't get swept too far out into the blue. Divers normally just head out to the wall from the *Malayan* Wreck site and then follow a guide into blue water anywhere from 10ft to 82ft off the wall. If you're lucky, the school can be seen in clear water. The boat crew say there is about a 70% success rate during the season.

125	**TUBBATAHA SOUTH**

Location: *SW of Tubbataha's North Islet*
Depth: *0-130ft (0-40m)*
Access: *Live-aboard*
Range: *Intermediate*

There are many notable sites at the southern end of this reef system plus an old lighthouse that sits bravely on an inner-reef sandbar with trees, sea birds and bushes. The lighthouse is off limits to visitors, however, a fair while back the crew of the *Delsan* (now a nearby wreck) once spent weeks that turned into months here waiting to be rescued.

Delsan Point and the area heading south past Staghorn Point and South

ported to frequent this area near the end of the diving season, in May and June.

There is a dark rock exposed at low tide in the south of the area that has spawned dive sites named **Black Rock**, **South Wall**, **North Wall** and **T-Wreck**. When there are currents here, they attract a good population of sharks and other pelagics. Keep an eye out in the blue for schooling gray reef sharks. This area is known for its manta-ray sightings and its currents attract all kinds of fish from bigeye jack schools to the occasional tiger shark. The corals all along this part of the south are healthy and large. Big sea fans, sponges, garden-like arrays of soft corals and brilliant tube corals share the wall with red-fang surgeonfish and pyramid butterflyfish. Look under ledges and in the cracks and crevices for cleaning action, resting pufferfish and bigeye soldierfish.

Ko-ok is a bit farther down and beautiful in places. It is good for jacks and barracuda and has a sheer wall with golden and square spot anthias. There's lots of healthy hard coral in shallow water along the upper reef. This area is good for long dives and fascinating snorkeling.

Wall is a popular and prolific site that produces sightings of cool pelagic life like spinner dolphin pods and whale sharks in almost every diving season. There's an area called the **Valley** in that is marked by sea whips – it is in here that the big guys are seen. Look for the large marble rays that consistently move through here. Gray reef sharks can also be seen in deeper water off this large bowl. If there is some southern-moving current, drop in north of the *Delsan* for the most fish life, such as rainbow runners and blackbar and yellowtail barracuda and bigeye jacks.

The shallows and sandy upper reef is called **Staghorn** but some have suggested a name change to Turtle Town. Multiple green and sea turtles can be seen here, especially on the afternoon dives. Approach slowly. The turtles are usually grazing before getting ready to sleep so you can get close and easily watch them. Manta rays are also re-

Pygmy seahorse

The Tubbataha Rangers

The guardians of Tubbataha are perched precariously on a sandbar on South Tubbataha, their patrol boats moored in a shallow natural channel. Here as many as 14 volunteers from various organizations, such as WWF, work and take turns patrolling the area to keep it free of poachers.

In December 1999, the foundation was rebuilt and the station, which sits high on stilts because its sandbar disappears at high tide, has seen various additions ever since. It does offer some protection but it must be a bit worrisome during major storms. There is a small victory garden, chickens are occasionally brought out and the rangers are the only people allowed to legally catch fish in this Unesco World Heritage site.

Rangers stay here for about three months at a time and also greet visiting divers and raise some funds by selling T-shirts. The Tubbataha Reefs is the only Unesco World Heritage site in Asia that is marine in nature. Park-access fees are used to manage, maintain and improve the park as well as financing law enforcement and education campaigns, facilities, boat maintenance and ranger training.

Returning to the live-aboard

Hazardous Marine Life

Blackbar barracuda

The diversity of marine life in the Philippines extends to dangerous marine animals too. Most of these are quite small and not ferocious, but highly venomous. There are cone shells, stonefish, scorpionfish, stingrays, hydroids, fire corals, urchins and many other things that can adversely affect a diver. Divers should read or ask about which will be commonly seen, and know first-aid procedures. Carrying proper antiseptic ointments greatly helps. Be especially careful on night dives.

SHARKS

Sharks are encountered on a few dives in the Philippines. Sadly, the shark-fin trade has thinned their number on the reefs. Most that are seen are puppylike reef whitetips. Attacks are rare and usually only occur in some misguided feeding attempt or to fishermen spearing fish. In the event a shark does become aggressive, it is sometimes wise to rise to a shallower depth to get out of its territory. If it comes too close, stop and face the animal and watch it closely and quietly. Be prepared to push it away with a camera, knife, spear or tank. In

the event of a bite, stop any bleeding, reassure the patient, treat for shock and seek immediate medical treatment.

FIRE CORAL

It looks pretty with its caramel color, but it is like putting your hand on a cigarette. It actually has tiny 'hairs' containing powerful nematocysts that will make your skin burn and itch like crazy and swell up afterward, if you touch them. This mechanism is to defend against munching parrotfish but divers sometimes get tagged as well. In the event of a sting, rinse with sea- or fresh water and apply vinegar or methylated alcohol to the affected area. In a severe case, antihistamines can help, but seek immediate medical treatment.

JELLYFISH

The stings of a jelly are released by nematocysts contained in the trailing tentacles. The rule of thumb is the longer the tentacles, the more painful the sting. Keep an eye out for jellyfish in the open water at decompression levels of 10ft to 25ft and while snorkeling. Deeper, drifting pelagic jellies are sometimes seen, and usually easily avoided. Most stings can be treated with vinegar. Some people do react adversely to jellyfish stings, similar to those who are allergic to bee stings. Be prepared to administer CPR and seek medical aid.

BARRACUDA

Barracuda bites are also quite rare and again, usually associated with some misguided feeding attempt. The fish tend to be attracted to shiny objects and have been known to attack in murky water. Such as with sharks, this is normally a case of mistaken identity and invariably an accident. On the Philippines' reefs, schools and individual blackbar barracuda can be encountered. There are also a few of the larger great barracuda. These fish should not be teased. Their bites can be damaging – stop any bleeding, reassure the patient, treat for shock and seek immediate medical treatment.

STONEFISH/SCORPIONFISH/ LIONFISH

These fish will be seen commonly in sandy and rubbly areas in the Philippines' waters where critter photography and muck diving is popular. They are often also out on night dives. They inject their venom with spines on their back, and the wound can be quite painful, with a lot of swelling. To treat, wash the wound, immerse in water as hot as the victim can stand for 60 to 90 minutes and seek medical aid.

SEA URCHINS

These spiny critters can be a real problem. The stings from their spines can range from irritating to highly intense. Spines can also break off inside the skin. Avoid contact – this means being vigilant in the areas they frequent, especially at night. Seek medical advice and use antibiotics where advised. Spines may have to be surgically removed, but in most cases they break up and work their way out of the skin over time.

Lionfish

CORAL FACTS Dee Scarr

- We use the word 'coral' for three things: the individual coral animal, called the polyp; the polyps and the skeleton they've secreted, also called a coral head; and the skeleton without its living polyps, also called coral rock. The first two of these are alive; the last is not, which leaves a great deal of room for confusion.
- A coral polyp (the living coral animal) is only three to four cell layers thick – as thin and fragile as a wet tissue draped across a razor blade.
- Every individual coral animal in a coral head is a clone of every other coral animal in that coral head.
- A coral head is started by a single coral larva, which grows and begins to secrete a calcium-based skeleton, clones itself and repeats the process. Slowly.
- A hemispherical coral head 3ft across is 200 to 300 years old.
- The branching corals, elkhorn and staghorn, grow more quickly than the 'head' corals, such as brain coral and star coral. They thrive in shallower waters, though, so are more likely to be broken by wave action.
- Look at a star coral head, or a starlet coral head: every single little mound or indentation – every single little circle in the whole coral head – is an individual coral animal.
- Look at a brain coral head, or a sheet coral: the polyps aren't as easy to distinguish as they are in the star corals, but a careful look will reveal the mouths of the polyps, daytime or nighttime.
- The tissue of every coral polyp in a coral head is connected to all the polyps around it. The entire surface of a coral head is covered with living coral tissue.

Travel Facts

A crowded tricycle

GETTING THERE

Many international airlines service the Philippines on a daily basis, so most people come in through Manila's Ninoy Aquino International Airport or Cebu City's Mactan-Cebu International Airport. Subic Bay also has an international airport. You can find very reasonable fares to/from Manila from many Asian and international destinations.

To hop around from dive venue to dive venue, domestic Philippine Airlines (PAL), Cebu Pacific Air and a handful of others have connecting flights at the Ninoy Aquino International Airport.

One oddity is that everything pretty much goes through this main hub one trip at a time. For instance, if you want to fly from Legaspi to Puerto Princesa, you will have to get your bags in Manila after your Legaspi leg and check-in again for the Puerto Princesa flight even if you are on the same airline. Your bags won't be checked through to your next destination and you won't receive a boarding pass for your onward destination. Schedule accordingly to give yourself time for this.

Airlines do weigh everything and the flights are pretty reasonable, but overweight charges are strict. Pack accordingly – 20kg is about all you get for most flights.

For divers, it is best to pre-arrange a package with a hotel and dive shop to include transfers and airport pick-up as well. This cuts down on the headaches of making travel arrangements in country and assures a confirmed seat. The internet booking services of both PAL and Cebu Pacific Air are also very handy.

Cebu Pacific Air even allows advance purchase of extra baggage weight, which is cheaper online than if you have to pay at the counter. Cebu Pacific Air can also be entertaining – it has quizzes in-flight and gives out small prizes for the right answer!

You have to pay a departure tax when leaving Manila, whether domestic or international. The cost is P550 for international departure and P100 for local departure (paid in Philippine pesos only). However, departing passengers for international destinations should check with airport or tourist information counters (☎ 524 1703, 832 2964) because the amounts may change without notice.

December is a busy local travel period. Book in advance, especially over the holiday periods when kids are out of school – family vacations are a big deal in the Philippines.

ENTRY REQUIREMENTS

Both adults and children require passports that are valid at least six months beyond their date of entry into the Philippines and also a return ticket or some proof of exit transport from the Philippines. Except for stateless persons and those from countries with which the Philippines has no diplomatic relations, all visitors may enter the country without visas and may stay for 21 days, provided they have tickets for an onward journey. Holders of Hong Kong and Taiwan passports must have special permits. Visas and special permits may be obtained from Philippine embassies and consulates.

GETTING AROUND

You'll experience the Philippines' transport and travel flow right off. And it's pretty safe to say you may find by the end of your trip you have used modes of transportation you've never tried before. People get around using bikes, motorbikes, pedal cabs, powered tricycles, jeepneys, cabs, vans, limos, all sizes

Glassy Sulu Sea

of outrigger bangka, powerboat, cabin cruiser, public ferry, propjet, commercial jet and air bus… just to name a few. You can also walk.

You can arrange for transport between your hotel and the airport through your hotel or dive shop. In most cases, you'll get a nice van or car that has plenty of room for dive gear, and air-con.

Once at the hotel, you may want to explore a bit. Getting to a town or to dinner you can use the 'Philippine rickshaw' or tricycle. It's a motorbike with a sidecar. They can be colorfully painted and look great (or not) but rarely have good shocks. Tricycles are found in their various forms nearly everywhere and are used for short trips. In many areas, they can also be rented with a driver by the hour.

The brave can also rent a car, but driving Philippine-style is a skill all of its own. Think hard about this before taking the plunge. Philippine law requires that you have a minimum of P750,000 third-party auto insurance with a Philippines auto-insurance company (available from local insurance agencies) when you drive in the Philippines. If you rent a car, this can be arranged with the rental agency.

TIME

The Philippines is in zone GMT+8, or the same as Hong Kong and Perth, Australia. The Philippines does not change time for daylight saving.

MONEY

The Philippine peso (P) is the country's official currency. Most tourist-oriented businesses accept major credit cards, traveler's checks and cash. But check ahead as there are some places that are cash only, with ATMs nowhere to be found.

There are ATMs around all of the major cities but many are only for local Philippine banks and, oddly, some accept Visa or MasterCard only, not always both. As for money changers, if you're offered a very good exchange rate, you're probably being set up. Change money at banks or accredited exchange facilities.

Money changers will be able to give you the official guiding rates and are located at the airport, local banks and other authorized foreign-exchange dealers in commercial establishments.

It is best to have some cash for purchases, hotel rooms and food on the small islands.

Tax

Sale of goods and other properties, services and importation of goods, are subject to 12% VAT. VAT is imposed on the gross selling price (in the case of sale of goods) and gross receipts (in the case of services). But this is mostly found in big cities, in places such as malls. Most small stores, food stands and markets just charge a flat price.

Tipping

Tipping is expected for many services, especially for porters, bellboys, waitpersons and other light services. The standard practice is to tip 10% of the total bill. Tipping is optional on bills that already include a 10% service charge.

ELECTRICITY

Most major cities in the Philippines have reasonably reliable power. However, in the provinces and on islands it can be a different matter. Some places have intermittent outages and some have planned outages. This can be tough when you have to charge your camera, strobe or dive light on a daily basis. Choose a resort with a generator if this could be a problem.

Power supplied on the national grid is supposed to be 220V/50Hz, but be warned that it frequently fluctuates between 190V and 250V, which can wreak havoc on sensitive equipment. Outlets accommodating two flat pins are standard throughout the country. Bring adapters and converters, because most outlets don't allow you to plug in the standard three-prong plugs. So you will need a power strip (power board) or single plug adapter for things to all work.

WEIGHTS & MEASURES

The Philippines officially uses the metric system, but old habits die hard and many measurements and distances are expressed using the imperial system. Most dive operators still refer to dive depths in feet and tank pressure in pounds per square inch. Much of the rental equipment is also set up this way.

INTERNET

E-mail outlets and internet cafés are becoming more and more prevalent, although they may lack a bit in speed in many places. If you are trying to use a local internet service, don't go when school is just out. The place will be packed with kids playing computer games.

Many of the hotels have computers centers and business centers, and a few even have wireless daily packages. A few of the cell-phone providers such as Smart and Globe offer USB-style wi-fi receivers that plug into your computer and are very effective when the wi-fi signal is strong. You can even do it while rolling down the highway in your taxi (but we don't recommend doing it from your tricycle). The signal strength varies quite a bit from locale to locale. But it allows you to use your own laptop for email and internet surfing and get internet in the more remote places such as Donsol or Malapascua that don't have internet cafés.

POSTAL

Local word is that the postal service is fairly reliable. Still, many folks use EMS, FedEx or DHL for anything valuable or something that needs a timely delivery.

There are private postal businesses that also advertise packing and shipping services. You can send those souvenirs that make your luggage overweight home with ease using EMS. For postcards, the local post office or your hotel front desk can mail them off for you.

A dedicated dive resort, the Bahura

ACCOMMODATION

There are hotels for every budget in the Philippines, and rooms, on the whole, are very affordable. Many dive destinations have budget cottages and rooms starting as low as US$20 per night, although there is now a trend toward very nice boutique dive resorts with private rooms or cottages from US$50.

Three-star hotels, found in many larger cities, start as low as US$18. Most top-end local hotels offer services and amenities similar to the popular international chains, typically at a cost of more than US$100 per night. Look into the packages because many resorts on private islands or nice shorelines often include diving and meals and cost from US$50 to $100 per night.

At the extreme top-end of the scale, exclusive resorts, such as Amanpulo, charge upward of US$750 to US$4300 per night.

The Department of Tourism has a homestay program that offers visitors the comfort of modest homes and an insight into Philippine life. For information, contact the **Tourist Information Center** (☎ 524 2384, 524 1703; Room 106, Department of Tourism Bldg, Manila).

DINING & FOOD

You may have to let out your welt belt a bit toward the end of your trip to the Philippines. Local cuisine is varied and tasty and there are many excellent restaurants featuring international fare. Local Filipino food borrows heavily from a mélange of cultures, especially Chinese and Malay. MSG is widely used, but if you don't want it in your food, you can tell the waiter 'walang vegin or walang ajinomoto tak tak tak.'

Don't pass up the chance to try lechon baboy, a spit-roasted pig served with a rich liver sauce. Another popular food to try is kilawin, called kinilaw in Cebu. It's made of raw fish, usually Spanish mackerel or tuna, marinated in local cane vinegar and coconut milk and spiced with small chilies, ginger and shallots. It's delicious, especially when eaten with an ice-cold San Miguel beer, one of the Philippines' most successful products.

SHOPPING

The big city malls, tourist gift shops and crafts centers, as well as local markets, offer all kinds of shopping opportunities. You can pick up a designer handbag, sunglasses or T-shirt at local markets for a couple of US dollars. Prices on handmade items such as carvings and weavings are normally very reasonable compared to other tourist destinations. Locally produced clothes and fashion accessories are real bargains. Filipinos

Shell & Coral Products

Regulations against the taking of shells, corals and natural artifacts are not very well enforced in the Philippines except at the major marine sanctuaries. So there are many items for sale incorporating shells and marine creatures. These can often be seen in the form of products such as bracelets and earrings. Most of the time, these are not harvested sustainably. Divers are encouraged to discourage the creation of these products by not purchasing such items and telling store owners that they disapprove of seeing these items on the shelves.

If you are offered a wildlife product or natural item for sale, ask questions about the product's origin. If the vendor seems poorly informed, think twice about your actions. Otherwise, your purchase could encourage continued illegal trade in wildlife, and be confiscated on your return home.

When in doubt, don't buy and don't take. Leave it.

make some very appealing intricate silverware, and Filipino costume jewelry is exported around the world.

While this is probably not the best place to shop for an expensive watch or top-end electronic product, you'll find a huge range of competitively priced international and local goods, some of which are cheaper here than at more obvious shopping capitals, such as Hong Kong.

ACTIVITIES & ATTRACTIONS

There are plenty of things to do in the Philippines besides diving. For those looking for a room with a view and some cool mountain breezes, try either Baguio as one of the country's favorite mountain retreats or Banaue, with its amazing rice terraces. The terraces are a Unesco World Heritage site that dates back 2000 years and are picture-perfect.

If you're headed south you can try jungle trekking in Palawan. The sparsely populated region has endemic flora and fauna. Kayaking around El Nido is also popular and the Puerto Princesa Subterranean River is another Unesco site. Here you can travel underground for about 3 miles while ducking swiftlets and listening to the screeches of bats.

At Cagayan de Oro you can try white-water rafting down the Cagayan River. Or if you just have a day in Manila, there's a day trip to the Tinglayen area for a look at the last of the Kalinga headhunters and their environs.

The Philippines has lots to do for outdoor activities plus historical tours, cultural tours and even cooking classes that include market visits to get the freshest foods for your culinary creations.

TOURIST OFFICES

For visitor information visit the Department of Tourism (DOT) website at www.wowphilippines.com.ph.

RECOMMENDED BOOKS

Anilao by Scott Tuason
Bahura by Scott Tuason

Giraffes in the RP? You bet in Palawan!

LISTINGS

Scuba surfing

THE PHILIPPINES DIVE OPERATORS

Selecting a Dive Operator

Dive operators in the Philippines are working to create a unified standard and high level of training for their divemasters and boat captains. The Philippine Commission on Sport Scuba Diving (PCSSD) tries to maintain high standards for membership, so tourists can feel secure. Personalized service is also coming to the fore. Thus, the chances of getting a poor or unsafe service are much less than they were a decade ago. Professional Association of Diving Instructors (PADI)– and Scuba Schools International (SSI)–accreditation agencies are also very active in the country ensuring safety standards are up-to-date and being met.

However, the Philippines' recent boom in tourism and the popularity of scuba diving means there are also a few shoestring operations where proper training and equipment maintenance is a secondary concern. For your own safety, peace of mind, value for the dollar and quality of holiday, it pays to be a wise consumer. Usually you get what you pay for – if a deal seems too good to be true, it probably is.

Get satisfactory answers about the operation you are planning to dive with, the type of equipment, the type of boat and its maintenance, the divemasters, insurance coverage, the cost of diving, ratio of divemasters to divers in the water, the knowledge of the travel agent you are booking with and any other details that may be important.

Check the internet as well. Most of the better dive operators have very extensive websites with lots of good information about their businesses and diving in their respective parts of the country. Send plenty of emails.

The following listed organizations are PCSSD-accredited establishments and/or PADI- or SSI-sanctioned dive shops.

METROPOLITAN MANILA

Cruise Island Adventure
info@cia.com.ph
www.cia.com.ph

Expedition Fleet Live-Aboards
info@expeditionfleet.com
www.expeditionfleet.com

Scuba World Inc
swdiver@manila.com.ph
www.scubaworld.com.ph

BATANGAS

Acacia Resort & Dive Center
info@acaciadive.com
www.acaciadive.com

Anilao Beach Club
rolleenabu@yahoo.com
www.anilaobeachclub.com

Anilao Community Divers, Inc
bruja@attglobal.net

Outrigger Resort
info@expeditionfleet.com
www.expeditionfleet.com

Pier Uno Resort
pierunoresort@pldtdsl.net
www.pierunoresort.com

Portulano Dive Resort
inquire@portulano.com
www.portulano.com

SSI College
tsonykim@paran.com
www.ssicollege.com

Striga de Mari
gbmay@attglobal.net

BOHOL

Alona Divers Scuba Dive Center
alonadivers@hotmail.com
www.alonadivers.de

Ananyana Beach Resort Corp - Dive Center
info@ananyana.com
www.ananyana.com

Aqua Journey Inc
info@aqua-journey.com
www.aqua-journey.com

Atlantis Alona Dive Paradise Inc
lena@atlantisdivecenter.com

Balicasag Island Dive Resort
inquiries@divephil.com
www.divephil.com/bohol/balicasa

Bituon Beach Resort
info@bituon.com
www.bituon.com

Blue Planet Diving Center
info@blue-planet-diving.com
www.blue-planet-diving.com

Bohol Sea Resort/Adventure Sports Inc
henryhoeppner@hotmail.com
henryhoeppner@yahoo.com
www.boholsearesort.com

Bohol Wonder Lagoon Dive Resorts & Beds
kintae63@hanmail.net

Cabilao Dive Center
dive@laestrella.ph
www.laestrella.ph

Deeper Dive Inc
hanbuty@hanmail.net
www.deeper.co.kr

Good Diveshop Tours Co Ltd
shinjik@mozcom.com

Nova Beach Resort Bohol Inc
novabeach@globelines.comp.ph
www.bohol.jp

Philippine Fun Diver Inc
info@boholfundiverss.com
www.boholfundivers.com

Philippine Islands Divers Services Inc
diving@phildivers.com
Jacques@phildivers.com
www.phil.divers.com

Prosafari Dive and Equipment Center
info@prosafaricenter.com

Scuba World Inc. - Bohol
bohol@scubaworld.com.ph
www.scubaworld.com.ph

Sea Explorers
alonabeach@sea-explorers.com
www.sea-explorers.com

Seaquest Dive Center
info@seaquestdivecenter.ph

Sierra Madre Divers
smd@mozcom.com,
info@polarisdive.com
laniletonin@sierramadreresort.com
www.sierramadreresort.com

BORACAY

Aqualife Divers Academy
contact@aqualife-divers.com

Blue Mango Dive Center
dustinpratt@gmail.com
www.boracaydive.com

Calypso Diving School International
info@calypso-asia.com
www.calypso-asia.com

DiveGurus Boracay
info@divegurus.com
www.divegurus.com

Fisheye Divers Corp
info@fisheyedivers.com
www.fisheyedivers.com

Island Staff Diving & Tour Shoppe, Inc
rachelmaxino@yahoo.com.ph

Scuba Champ Inc
webmaster@scubachamp.co.kr
www.scubachamp.co.kr

Scuba World Inc – Boracay
boracay@scubaworld.com.ph
www.scubaworld.com.ph

Sea Gaia Dive Resort
satobuddy305@hotmail.com

Sea World Dive Center
kimsoonsik@hotmail.com

Victory Divers
info@victorydivers.com
www.victorydivers.com

Watercolors Boracay Diving Adventures
info@watercolors.ph
www.watercolors.ph

White Beach Divers
info@whitebeachdivers.com
www.whitebeachdivers.com

White Blue Diving Service
chi@whiteblue.jp
www.whiteblue.jp

CAMIGUIN

Johnny's Dive 'N' Fun
info@johnnysdive.com
www.johnnysdive.com

CEBU

7 Seas Aquanauts
7seas@mozcom.com
www.7seas-cebu.com

Alegre Dive Station
dive@alegrebeachresort.com
www.alegrebeachresort.com

Angel Marine Underwater Diving Services
dive@angelmarine.info

Badian Hotel Resort & Spa
badianisla@aol.com
badianoffices@aol.com
www.badianhotel.com

Blue Abyss Dive Shop
Basdiot, Moalboal, Cebu
info@blueabyssdiving.com

Blue Coral Diving Tours Co Ltd
bluecoral@bluecoral.jp
www.bluecoral.jp

Cat Marine Sports
Datag, Maribago, Lapu-Lapu City
☎ 032-495 2324, 0916-390 5701

Cebu Dive Centre
info@cebudivecentre.com
www.cebudivecentre.com

Cebu El Acuario Dive Shop
elacuariocebu@hotmail.com,
chihiro_soehata@hotmail.com

Coral Point Dive House
dcoralpoint@yahoo.com

Dive Point Alcoy Seawater
tauchbasis@divepointalcoy.com
www.divepointalcoy.com

Fun & Sun Development Corporation
info@funsundivetravel.com
www.funsundivetravel.com

Fun Diving Ia Corporation
saojung@hotmail.com

Jetmaster Water Sports
jetmaster-icot@yahoo.com
www.jetmasterwatersports.com

KI Marine Sports Center
infos@cebucruising.com
www.cebucruising.com

Magic Island Dive Resort Inc
info@magicisland.nl
www.magicisland.nl

Marine Village Dive House
ariel@marinevillage.net
www.marinevillage.net

Ocean Globe Diving Shop
hondatakamitsu@hotmail.com

Oxygene Diving Services
info@kasaivillage.com
www.oxygenediving.com
www.kasaivillage.com

P C Divers
pcdivers@scubaworld.com.ph
www.scubaworld.com.ph

Pado's Camp Resort Inc.
www.padoresort-cnaver.com

PSQ Divers
psq@skyinet.net
www5c.biglobe.ne.jp/~psq

Pulchra – P & I Resorts Inc
info@pulchraresorts.com
www.pulchraresorts.com

San Remigio Marine Dive Center
sanremigio2002@yahoo.com

Savedra Dive Center
info@savedra.com
karl@savedra.com
www.savedra.com

Scotty's Dive Center
dive@divescotty.com
admin@divescotty.com
www.divescotty.com

Scuba Cebu Diving Co Ltd
info@mailscubacebu.com
www.scubacebu.com

Scuba Star Dive Service
www.scubastar-barracuda.com

**Scuba World, Inc – Punta Engano/
Cebu City**
jm@scubaworld.com.ph
www.scubaworld.com.ph

Sea Explorers
cebu@sea-explorers.com
www.sea-explorers.com

Seaquest Dive Center
info@seaquestdivecenter.ph
www.seaquestdivecenter.ph

Suny Dive Shop
Punta Engano, Lapu-Lapu City
☎ 032-238 8136

Tharsis Marine Sports
Bagumbayan, Maribago, Lapu-Lapu City
☎ 032-495 7698
jennes-tharsismarinesports@yahoo.com

Tropical Island Adventures
tiacebu@yahoo.com

Turtle Bay Dive Resort
turtlebaydiveresort@yahoo.com
www.turtlebaydiveresort.com

DUMAGUETE-NEGROS ORIENTAL

Artistic Diving
info@artisticdiving.com
www.artisticdiving.com

Atlantis Dive Resort
dumaguete@atlantishotel.com
www.atlantishotel.com

Atmosphere Resorts
Gabrielle@atmosphereresorts.com
Matthew@atmosphereresorts.com
www.atmosphereresorts.com

Bahura Resort & Spa (branch of Cruise Island Adventure)
frontoffice@bahura.com
www.bahura.com

Easy Diving
raphael@easydiving.ph
www.easydiving.ph

Matangale Alibuwag Dive Resort
mantadive@philcom.ph
www.matangale.com

People Dive
wind747@hotmail.com

Scuba Ventures Dumaguete
scubav@globelines.com.ph

Sea Explorers - Dauin
cebu@sea-explorers.com
www.sea-explorers.com

Sipalay Easy Diving & Beach Resort
diving@sipalay.com
www.sipalay.com

LEGASPI/DONSOL

Donsol Whaleshark Adventure Tours
reservations_donsol@yahoo.com
www.donsolwhaleshark.multiply.com

FunDive Asia DiveCentre
reservations_donsol@yahoo.com
donsolwhaleshark.multiply.com

Pacific Blue Mango Dive Center
dustinpratt@gmail.com
yoshi@pacificblue.jp
www.pacificblue.jp/en/center.htm

Prosafari
info@prosafari.com
www.prosafari.com

LUZON ISLAND

Dive Buddies Philippines
center@divephil.com

Divenet Philippines
info@divenetphil.com

Diver's Network
tom@diveph.com

Eureka Dive Inc.
eurekadive@eurekadive.com

Johan's Adventure & Wreck Dive Centre
johan@subicdive.com

MAKDiver
kiko.quinto@divefirm.com

Ocean Adventure & Camayan Beach Resort

snsharpe@oceanadventure.com.ph

Ocean Deep Diver Training Center
tim@oceandeep.biz

Outrigger – Scuba World Inc
info@expeditionfleet.com
www.expeditionfleet.com

Portulano Dive Resort
inquiry@portulano.com

Scuba World Inc - Makati City
sales@scubaworld.com.ph

Scuba World Inc - San Juan
aboy@scubaworld.com.ph

Sunbeam Marine Sports Corporation
info@anilao-sunbeam.com
www.anilaodivers.com

LEYTE

Sogod Bay Scuba Resort Inc
pmcguire@sogodbayscubaresort.com
www.sogodbayscubaresort.com

Southern Leyte Divers
info@leyte-divers.com

MALAPASCUA

**Divelink Cebu/
Malapascua Aquaports Corp.**
divelinkcebu@yahoo.com
www.divelinkcebu.com

**Malapascua Beach Resort and
Dive Shop**
info@bantiguecove.com
www.bantiguecove.com

Malapascua-Exotic Island Dive Resort
exoticdivers@gmail.com
Sea Explorers
malapascua@sea-explorers.com
www.sea-explorers.com

Thresher Shark Divers
dive@thresherdivers.com
www.thresherdivers.com

MINDANAO

Mantangale Alibuag Dive Resort Inc
mantadive@philcom.ph

Wind and Wave Davao
info@windandwavedavao.com

PALAWAN

Dugong Dive Center
info@dugongdivecenter.com
www.dugongdivecenter.com

Discovery Divers
info@ddivers.com
www.ddivers.com

Dive & Let Live
ponnetpeter@hotmail.com

Dive Calamanianes
info@divecal.com
www.divecal.com

Diving El Busero
☎ 48-433 6101

Dos Palmas Arreceffi Island Resort
info@dospalmas.com.ph
www.dospalmas.com.ph

El Nido Resorts
badriano@elnidoresorts.com
www.elnidoresorts.com

Eureka Dive in Pamalican Island
eurekadive@eurekadive.com
www.eurekadive.com

Sangat Island Reserve
(email form on website)
www.sangat.com.ph

SeaDive Resort
seadive@seadiveresort.com
www.seadiveresort.com

PUERTO GALERA/MINDORO

A B Wonder Dive
info@abwonderdive.com
www.abwonderdive.com

Action Divers
info@actiondivers.com
www.actiondivers.com

Asia Divers Dive Resort
El Galleon Dive Resort &
Hotel/Asia Divers
admin@asiadivers.com
www.asiadivers.com

Atlantis Beach Resorts & Dive Centers
info@atlantishotel.com
www.atlantishotel.com

Big Apple Dive Resort
divebigapple@gmail.com

Club Mabuhay Dive Resort
clubmabuhayresort@gmail.com
mabuhaysabang@hotmail.com
www.clubmabuhayresort.com

Coco Divers
thomas@cocodivers.com
www.cocodivers.com

Coral Cove Resort
info@coral-cove.com
www.coral-cove.com

Dive Dojo
paul@divedojo.com
www.divedojo.com

Diving Park
pmk3kr@yahoo.co.kr

La Laguna Dive Center
lalaguna@llbc.com.ph

Marco Vincent Dive Resort
grace@mvdive.com
www.marcovincent.com

Mermaid Resort
info@mermaidresort.com
www.mermaidresort.com

Octopus Divers Inc
info@octopusdivers.org
www.octopusdivers.org

Paradise Dive Resort
diver_ricky@hotmail.com

Red Sun Dive Resort
redsundiver@hotmail.com
www.redsunresort.com

Sabang Beach Club
musso4115@yahoo.co.kr

Scandinavian Divers Inc
info@scandinaviandivers.com
www.scandinaviandivers.com

Scuba World Inc – Puerto Galera
pg@scubaworld.com.ph
www.scubaworld.com.ph

Seaview Divers – White Beach
tim_losper@yahoo.com

Song of Joy Resort
texsong2001@yahoo.co.kr
www.songofjoyresort.com

South Sea Divers
dive@southseadivers.com
www.southseadivers.com

**Tech Dive IT Academy
International**
simon@techdiveit.com
www.techdiveit.com

Tropicana Dive Resort
paultropicana@yahoo.com
www.tropicanadivers.com

LIVE-ABOARDS

**Atlantis Azores/
Atlantis Dive Resorts - Philippines**
reservations@atlantishotel.com
www.atlantishotel.com/liveaboard/
Index.php

**Dugong Dive Center/
Paradise Island, Dimyaka**
info@dugongdivecenter.com
www.dugongdivecenter.com

Expedition Fleet Live-Aboards
info@expeditionfleet.com
www.expeditionfleet.com

MV Eagle 5
charter@eagleoffshore.com.ph
www.eagleoffshore.com.ph

Worldwide Dive and Sail
info@worldwidediveandsail.com
www.worldwidediveandsail.com

Index

THIS IS NOT
THE END

lonely

CHAT TO TRAVELLERS · GIVE US FEEDBACK · GET EXTRA DESTINATION
INFORMATION · BOOK FLIGHTS, ACCOMMODATION AND EVERYTHING
ELSE · PLAN TRIPS · GIVE ADVICE · LISTEN IN · FIND, BUY AND SELL
THINGS · SHARE STORIES · MAKE A CONNECTION · AND MORE